I0054344

# RAISE YOURSELF FROM DEBT TO WEALTH

Eliminate Debt, Improve Wealth, Build Credit

Rev. Dr. K. Bill Dost

Copyright © 2020 by Rev. Dr. K. Bill Dost

All rights reserved. No part of this publication may be reproduced, distributed, or transmitted in any form or by any means, including photocopying, recording, or other electronic or mechanical methods, without the prior written permission of the author, except in the case of brief quotations embodied in critical reviews and certain other noncommercial uses permitted by copyright law. For permission requests, write to the author at the address below.

ISBN: 978-1-951503-28-4 (Ebook)
ISBN: 978-1-951503-27-7 (Paperback)

\\\\ AUTHORSUNITE

Published by Authorsunite.com

# CONTENTS

# Introduction

**Why did I write this book?**

I got tired—tired of people defaulting on their credit, tired of having to pursue customers because they didn't understand what they were signing, what they were doing to their credit and their ability to service debt. And I was tired that educated people were drowning in debt and didn't know what to do about it except give up.

I also got tired of people preying on the poor, those with poor credit, the elderly, the uninformed, and then those people becoming the talking points of a government that tried to solve a problem without actually looking into what was happening to people. The clarion call became getting rid of high-rate credit providers, without checking into what they were doing. Instead of finding a way for those who required higher-rate credit to get it in an affordable manner, it became more important to put those companies under high levels of compliance and government oversight, or simply make it unaffordable for them to stay in business, thereby leaving the end-user client without an option other than paying a visit to "Guido" in the back of the pub.

Finally, I was tired of people losing hope, of feeling shame and that there was no way out. Life had dealt them a blow and they simply couldn't seem to get back on the right side of their debt or their credit. It seemed the only option was to simply give up. Sadly, I've seen this so many times, and the ensuing guilt and shame that comes with it. Oddly enough, when you've lost it all, pride has a funny way of showing up and making you feel like you can't talk about what's going on or seek help when you need it most.

I wrote this book for those people, and maybe for you, if you have ever felt ashamed or angry because you feel like you deserve better credit than what you are being rated at, haven't been able to understand your credit, or if you feel like you've been drowning in debt and are looking for a way out. This book is your way out. This book lays out your path. But understand there is no short cut and no magic bullet. What it takes is a lot of hard work to make it happen. But the good news is that you *can* get out of debt, you *can* repair your credit, and you *can* save yourself a nice nest egg if you make a series of simple adjustments.

When I started what eventually became DND Finance, our goal was to help people at a grass-roots level. It eventually became a vehicle to change the lives of 1,000,000 entrepreneurs. As a lending company in what was originally commercial lending and now consumer lending, it's become more important to see people making better credit decisions.

It's a sad truth that most people don't have any savings—as few as eight percent in major western economies. This means if you miss just three paychecks you're bankrupt and underwater, regardless of how strong your credit may be.

It's another sad truth that most people have massive amounts debt, and far more credit card debt than could have ever been conceived in the past or that was acceptable. I know people who can't afford groceries unless it is on credit until next month—and I myself was that person at one point in my life!

It's also a sad truth that if you do have savings, or lower debt, you can still have a bad credit rating! It seems these ratings don't often go together. I've known the richest broke people in my life who can't seem to requalify for their mortgage, let alone purchase something new.

Credit, savings, and a solid rating is a balancing act you *can* master, and it's possible with simple and proven tips I myself used when I was younger. I have shown other people how to use these tips and strategies, and I know if you really follow the plan in this book, you can achieve a debt-free good credit rating as well.

I have put my more than twenty-five years of experience into this book, and I truly hope it will offer you the key insights you need to fix your credit, reduce your debt load, and help you make some positive changes in your financial future.

Welcome to the Tribe of the Undefeated!

## CALL TO ACTION

Go to www.scorebydnd.com/debttowealth and sign up for our blog where you will get tips and tricks that will support you through this book. In addition, if you email debttowealth@ scorebydnd.com, we'll send you worksheets that also go along with this book free of charge!

# Part I

## Credit, Credit Reports, and Credit Repair

# 1

# Who Am I?

It's an interesting question, however I don't mean it in the esoteric or soul-searching way we often ask ourselves about. I simply mean it as a way to explain why I should be able to write a book telling you about debt, credit, and lending—and how to fix it.

You can read the front cover of this book, so you can see my name. But who am I? A brief history of my time on this Earth is in order. My name is Bill Dost and I run a company called DND Finance. You can also see I am a Rev. Dr.—well what is that? It's a fancy way of saying I went to theology school, got a doctorate degree, and was eventually ordained into the ministry. It also means that, hopefully, I have a social care or desire to help other people—which in fact I do. We've always run our business and our lives in the pursuit of helping other people. That doesn't mean I don't like nice things, I just believe it's more interesting if we all have the chance to succeed and live and have things like food, shelter and luxuries like a home. I don't believe there has to be "haves" and "have-nots." I more believe there are those who are willing to work, and those who are not. But I digress.

In the year 2000 I opened a company that eventually became DND Finance. DND had one goal, which is to change the lives of 1,000,000 entrepreneurs. That didn't come naturally; it occurred over time and mainly because we realized how entrepreneurs, a subset of the greater whole, still had issues like marriage problems, money problems, and other life problems, just like you and me. When people think of entrepreneurs, they often think of high-profile people like Richard Branson, Steve Jobs, and Elon Musk. But for each one of them there are literally scores of entrepreneurs who have failed or only achieved a small modicum of success but still have issues that need ironing out. This book serves to help work on one of those challenges—the one around money, debt, credit, savings, and lending.

DND Finance is a lending company in Canada, the UK, and the USA. You can learn tons about us at www.dndf.business. For the purpose of this book, it's important to understand DND lends money for equipment purchases for your business, provides working capital loans for your companies, and both personally and corporately offers a charge card product. This means we have seen many credit profiles, both consumer and commercial, over the course of the last two decades we have been in existence. Unfortunately, many of the credit profiles we see are on the weaker side, due to the fact we serve what is called the "near prime" and "sub-prime" market places. These are markets where traditional lenders refuse or are unable to provide finance. It means we take higher risks on customers and have a higher incidence of those customers going bankrupt, having problems, or simply not being able to make good on their contracts than our colleagues in the industry who don't look at deals in our niche.

My experience comes from more than twenty years of looking at credit profiles and financial statements, making credit decisions, and seeing how those decisions have played out. It's also borne out in my own personal life. At the age of eighteen I got my first credit card, racked up $5,000 dollars in debt and had to take out a loan to service it and yet GOT TO KEEP THE CARD. I didn't learn proper credit behavior for years, and my credit, and my driving record, took a beating until I was twenty-one. At that point I got myself straight and slowly paid off all my debt and kept it that way. In twenty-plus years I've had one speeding ticket (and almost lost my driving privileges between ages sixteen and twenty-one), and with the exception of a rough patch later in life, have kept virtually no credit card debt most of my life.

I'd like to say my parents taught me that and to a degree they did. But it was also the core principles I learned on how to get out of debt, how to save money, and how to correct my credit profile. I know there are other books on how to do this, but in my opinion I think they have gotten it slightly wrong. Some will tell you don't worry about your credit while you pay off your debt, which could be a seven-year mistake I'll explain to you later. Others will tell you to pay off your debt before saving any money for the future, due to interest rate arbitrage, but the problem there is you may have nothing for a rainy day, for your retirement, or for celebrating your victories, which may lead to relapse. I know what you're thinking: What do you mean celebrate? I'll get to that later in the book as well. But I wrote this book based on my personal experience and what I have seen for years in my industry, all colored through the lens that I really and truly care about *you* as a person. It's the minister thing in me. If you want more history than this on me, there is another book I wrote before this one about marriage you could get your hands on. And it'll help me save some money as well!

# 2

# Household Debt

You don't have to go further than a quick google search to note that household debt levels are reaching what are being called record highs. In my native Canada, when looking at the average Canadian, for every dollar of income a Canadian earns after taxes, they owe $1.70. This is a household debt level of 170 percent of disposable income! And this is up from about 100 percent twenty years ago. This is a statistic from the Bank of Canada from May 2018.[1]

In the USA, back in August 2018, Reuters reported household debt rose to $13.3 trillion, which was up $454 billon from the previous year, making it the sixteenth consecutive quarter of increases according to the New York Federal Reserve.[2]

And in the UK, average household debt now stands at a record £15,400 owed to credit card firms, banks, and other lenders according to the TUC (Trades Union Congress) as reported by the guardian. This is a combined £428 billion in the third quarter of 2018. This means each household owed £886 more than it did twelve months before that. The level of debt

---

[1] See https://www.bankofcanada.ca/2018/05/canada-economy-household-debt-how-big-the-problem/

[2] See https://www.reuters.com/article/us-usa-fed-debt/u-s-household-debt-rises-to-13-3-trillion-in-second-quarter-idUSKBN1KZ1QZ

as a share household income is now at 30.4 percent, which is the highest it's ever been. As a comparison, it is above the £286 billion at the peak of 2008 right before the credit crisis.[3]

I could go on and on and mention many more countries, but I think you get the point. The reality is our countries, and likely the whole world, are in serious trouble. We are in over our head when it comes to debt, and we clearly aren't managing our credit levels well enough. I know this because I look at credit on a daily basis, or at least my team does.

This is why most reports you hear or read about openly state how most people are only one or a few paychecks away from being in serious trouble. This means if you missed two paychecks you could end up losing cars, homes, and more. This isn't necessarily accurate, however, as the knock-on effect would cause such irreparable damage you might not ever recover from it! Most credit providers will give you at least ninety days of missed payments before they take any action (more on that later), but just because you scramble and make the payment doesn't mean you will make it through and get caught up.

Household debt is clearly out of control, and If that's the case, then what hope is there? We're hopelessly drowning in debt as a nation, but what are we supposed to do as a nation when it comes to getting out of debt, not to mention managing our credit and keeping it clean?

What happens if the wheels come off and we miss a couple of those paychecks? The answer comes down to either door number one or two: We either wipe out our savings, or we max out our debt.

---

[3]  See https://www.theguardian.com/business/2019/jan/07/average-uk-household-debt-now-stands-at-record-15400

Then again, according to most statistics, the incidence of money being saved is almost nil, so there really isn't a door number one at all. But that's okay because there is door number two. Umm, actually there is no door number two either, because according to the stats from above we're already maxed out on our credit cards. What happens if we miss a paycheck then? Is there a door number three? The short answer is NO.

Yes, we drown in debt, then we get depressed, and then we quit. Ultimately, we go bankrupt if it's bad enough and we can't recover, and if we have to make mortgage or rent payments, plus our credit card payments, plus utilities, food, and anything else, and we have no income, it's pretty easy to see that the card payments will stop and the cards will be maxed. That's a short-term solution to a very long-term problem—with very few solutions for coming back out of it.

# 3

# What Happens When It Goes Wrong

The world is a great and scary place. And unfortunately, being in the industry I am in, which is higher-risk lending, I have had the opportunity to see what happens both when things go right and when things go wrong. The sad truth is, things go wrong more than we want to believe. If your credit cards are maxed and you don't have savings, what are you going to do when you lose your paycheck, or a smaller issue arises, such as your child needs braces, or your car needs a new engine? You're in trouble.

But Bill, you may say, I pay the minimum monthly balance on my credit card and I can increase my borrowing when I need it. Yes, that can work for a short period of time. It also means you are behind the curve. It means if you keep doing that and not paying down your credit card, that your credit will take a beating over time. That is something you don't want to happen—you want to protect your credit rating as much as you can.

Here's the reality check: When the wheels come off and things go wrong, you will likely be in big trouble. I want to address this at the start because if we can't be honest with ourselves now, in the beginning, then the rest of this book is a wasted read. Ask yourself, or better yet, write down on paper what would happen if you missed one paycheck, two paychecks, and three paychecks. This only works if you write out your costs on one side and your income on the other, and for bonus points separate your must-have costs on one side and your disposable costs underneath as a separate section. Examples of each include insurance for the car, which is a must have cost, and cable on your television, which is a disposable cost.

Go do the exercise listed in the Call to Action at the end of this chapter and then come back here.

I suspect you'll find you have a limited income and a number of costs, and of the costs you've got the must-haves, such as mortgage or rent payment, car payment, heat, and the "nice-to-haves," such as cable, Netflix, and so on. Most will find they can cut a few costs if the going gets tough, but for the most part, many of those costs they could cut they either won't be able to make the decision quite fast enough to be helpful (cable, the gym, and any many others take thirty days advance notice to cancel), or they won't realize how much trouble they are in and simply won't cancel some subscriptions. After all, Netflix is only $9.99, Spotify is only $9.99, Amazon Prime is only $8.99, and cable is only $49.99. Taken separately, each of these are small costs, but taken together they may amount to nearly $80 a month, which is close to $1,000 a year, and they are *unnecessary*. The problem is that when things go wrong, $80/month may not help us, but $1,000 or $5,000 in the bank *could* make a substantial difference if push came to shove. Understanding your complete monthly expenditures will be a sobering wakeup call—that $5 Starbucks every day on the way to work ends up being $25 a week, $100 a month and $1,200 a year! Little expenditures DO accumulate into substantial amounts, and it's very important you get a handle on what is going where.

Now that you know what your monthly expenditures are, ask yourself what happens if you miss one paycheck? The small costs won't be an issue, the credit cards likely won't be an issue, but you'll need to have enough available credit on them to buy food and pay for essentials if you don't have savings. What if you miss a second month? Now bill collectors will be calling, your credit cards won't be thrilled you have missed their payment but may let you skate by, and rent or mortgage will be chasing you. If you miss a third paycheck, though? Most card companies will pause your card, cable, and internet, and what I would call the nice-to-have costs will cancel their services, and your landlord or bank will be having a serious talk with you about leaving your residence or making some payments, depending on where you live.

Without any safety net, and with most of your cards out of commission due to not being paid, you could find yourself in real trouble. If by some miracle you are able to secure a new paycheck even within a time period of sixty or ninety days, you will still have a hard road ahead of you. This is because you are so behind on payments for everything.

So how do you get caught up? You can't skip paying for heat one month, or skip paying for food one month. You could potentially cut those disposable costs we mentioned, but that will only go so far in keeping you afloat. Your rent or mortgage has to get caught up, as does your phone bill and internet bill, otherwise the services will simply be turned off. And now you are paying interest on your late payments, and you might find the credit cards that got you through are now causing more problems due to the increase in debt servicing costs (the interest on your credit cards), which makes paying things down seem impossible. This all adds up to still being in trouble, and in a very real way. Sadly, most who find themselves in this circumstance, without some real intervention and help, may not ever recover. This is where debt consolidation firms make their bread and butter. They help you move from many payments you cannot afford to make, to one large payment you can only HOPE to make. However, as I have friends who have been in this industry, they can help you out when used correctly as an intermediary between you and your creditors to negotiate a payment plan to keep you afloat.

However, whether you take this approach or not there are some real risks. When you go to one of these firms, or if you don't and you simply can't see your way through, all along the way your troubles are being reported to the credit bureaus and your credit report is taking a beating. Unfortunately, this means that those who lend you money and who base your ability to repay on your past usage of credit will look at your credit history, and if they find it isn't up to snuff, they will stop giving you credit or start to reduce your credit rating and thus your access to credit facilities. This is when your $5,000 card with a $6,000 balance sends you a letter saying you need to get caught up, and will also start reducing your line of credit, say to $4,000 because your credit profile doesn't support the level of credit you currently have.

As you can imagine, having slow payments, missed payments, or if you throw in the towel because you simply can't continue under the credit burden and declare bankruptcy, all have some serious implications for you. And so does negotiating with your creditors. All of these items have long, and I mean *long-term* consequences, for your credit profile, not to mention your debt facilities.

## CALL TO ACTION

Go to www.scorebydnd.com/debttowealth and enter the code exercise1 to complete the form and download the free worksheet from our website.

# 4

# How Long is Long?

In other words, for how long have I destroyed my credit?

If you have been living on your credit cards in the above example and have seen your credit rating go down, that's because you have been over-utilizing your credit or you have been (in the terms of the credit agency) *irresponsible* with your credit facilities. It's important to know how long certain decisions can stay on your credit profile.

In the UK, consumers are able to return their car loans under certain circumstances back to the original vendor and with the dealer's help at what they believe is no penalty. This typically happens towards the end of the term of the agreement, usually within ninety days of the end of the term, and usually the dealer will move them to a different car. The understanding is that the customer cannot be penalized or that it's a contractual right. What I learned, however, from a few of the credit analysts who worked at these car firms is that while this may be dealer-led, the firms themselves did not like losing their last three payments just because the dealer wanted to sell a better, newer, flashier car to the customer. In all cases, I've been informed that the interest rate or other credit factors would be "adjusted" in order to make up the lost revenue. The customer would also have an internal black mark on their record for the return, even though they thought it was "penalty-free," so while it wouldn't stop them from being approved for future credit, it could make that credit more expensive or the terms less desirable for the customer (shorter terms , higher down payment requirements, and so on). Companies will do anything to protect the firm. This is a known form of business practice called a Voluntary Termination. It then stands to reason that if you, for example, negotiate a lower term or different rate or structure for your credit facility, it *will* affect your credit and your credit rating. While the government legislation states your credit score cannot be affected, the actual finance companies will either find a way to not lend to you again, or will lend to you with less favorable terms.

If you go to a credit consolidator, which is one of the last-resort steps you might take in order to stave off bankruptcy, they will make similar proposals to your creditors, and it will seriously affect your credit standing. You are basically telling those you have borrowed from that you cannot pay them as agreed and that you need to renegotiate the terms. Often, your accounts will be noted as being in default until the consolidator has paid up for you, and the effect of paying up via the consolidator will show you were irresponsible with your ability to borrow. Everyone will know who you borrowed money from and see you couldn't make good on your agreements as originally made. This will stay on your credit report for a minimum of three to five years, if not even longer and dependent on how long it takes to pay off the credit.

A simple late payment, although one late payment may not be held against you, shows on your credit report for up to twenty-four months, and if you miss a payment it will show up on your report for eighteen to twenty-four months in the history section. That Visa payment of $69.90 you missed in January because things were tight? Even though you made it up later in March, it will be held against you and will be noted on your credit file for years to come. People will see you missed a payment, and often the amount of the missed payment.

Finally, bankruptcy (for those who think it may be their salvation), will not just reset your credit to a status as if you had none, the bankruptcy will be on your file for at least six years (in Canada and the UK for a first bankruptcy) and seven years for the USA after you are discharged. However, if you didn't make any payments towards your debts (in the USA) or it's a second bankruptcy, this number can increase to as much as 10 years (USA) or 14 years (Canada). Meaning, it will be extremely difficult to apply and be approved for any sort of credit facility that isn't termed "high risk," which could mean interest rates of 30% or more for years after your bankruptcy decision. While there are perfectly legitimate reasons to declare bankruptcy, I'd highly recommend you do everything in your power to avoid this route if at all possible. Except in very specific situations, it will put your financial life on full stop for years.

For the sake of completeness, any judgements you may have against you, meaning if Visa, or your bank, or a collection agency had to pursue you for funds, it will show up on your credit report and will be visible there for years to come. You want to avoid these situations if at all possible.

My point in telling you all this, and I'm extremely sorry for being the bearer of extremely bad news, is to make sure you understand that when things go bad, they go bad for a long time. My hope is to help you avoid having things go bad, to help you prevent this from happening by showing you how to navigate through the what-ifs and get your credit and savings set up in such a way that not only will you have a good rating, but you will be able to weather the storm of a missed paycheck, or at least know how to behave when it happens.

# 5

## Where Do You Want to Go?

When I do speaking engagements, I often ask the audience what the first part of planning a journey is. And it's not deciding where you want to go...it's acknowledging where you actually are right now. If you are desiring to go on holiday to New York City, you can't decide how to get there (plane, train, or automobile) until you can first accept where you are. Why? Because the ramifications of where you are will have an impact on planning your journey. If, for example you live in New Jersey, then traveling by car or train may be the way to go. If you live in Sydney, Australia, I'm afraid you're likely looking at an airplane. Without knowing where you are, you cannot even determine method of travel, your costs, your likely trip time, or anything else related to your trip. You must start by answering the question, where am I right now? Upon determining where you are, say Toronto, Canada, you can determine it's an eight-hour car ride, a very long train journey, or a simple 90-minute flight. From there you can count the cost of what it will take to go, such as how much time you need to take off, how long you want to be there, what kind of hotel to stay in, and so on.

Debt and credit are really no different. You need to know where you are and do a real assessment of your current situation. You might find you have three credit cards with $25,000 in debt, and a line of credit for another $30,000. You might also realize you have very little if any savings, and you wouldn't be alone. In the UK, more than 16 million individual adults have less than £100,[4] and one in four UK households have less than £95 in savings.[5] You might find that you pay your credit cards in a timely fashion and you are sitting at 50-60% usage on them. I encourage you to really sit down and write out a simple net-worth statement with a statement of income and outflows. This will be invaluable as you work through your debt-free plan. Go to the Call to Action at the end of this chapter to find out how to download the free resources and do this!

To walk you through the net worth statement, on the left input any of your assets (your house, your investments, your car) if you own them. Any extra items such as jewelry or art are tough to input, but for the sake of this, a good rule of thumb is that if you have it separately insured, you should write it down as an asset. So, anything you may own goes on the left. The cash value of your life insurance (not the insurance amount) can go here as well.

On the right-hand side is where you list what you owe. Your mortgage, any loans, lines of credit, and credit cards.

You then subtract the right side from the left side to calculate your net worth. This number then tells you how much your debt is eating into what you may own. You might have a $1,000,000 house, but if it has a mortgage of $500,000 and a home equity line of credit of $250,000 and you have $50,000 in credit card debt, there isn't much left over that can be called positive equity or net worth now is there?

---

[4]  See https://www.theguardian.com/society/2017/feb/20/one-in-four-uk-families-have-less-than-95-in-savings-report-finds.

[5]  See https://www.bbc.com/news/business-37504449.

The next statement you need to write down is all the income you have coming in, which is usually just your work income, but perhaps you have rental properties, or you have investments that pay you monthly. Whatever those are, put them on the left.

Your statement of outgoing (expenses or liabilities) money goes on the right-hand side. This could and would likely be the amount you pay against your credit cards, your mortgage, rent, utilities, insurance, car payment, and so on—anything that has a contractual agreement to it and that comes out of your resources each month goes in this list. If you have a monthly savings amount you put away, I would put that in there as well, along with all your bills such as cable, internet, phone bill, and so on.

At this point, hopefully you're outgoing isn't higher than your incoming. However, it is very possible that it is. If that's the case for you, I think you need to have a clear understanding of how much is coming in and how much is going out and then decide what do you really need? What is it that's an unnecessary drag on your income?

With both of these documents, you may be happy or you may be depressed, but the reality is you will *know* where you are. Without them, how can you truly say where you are in finances? Having a net-worth statement will allow you to know what is the long-term success or failure of your past decisions. The statement of cash flows (your incoming and outgoing) tells you exactly how far beyond or within your means you are living. With this, your eyes will be open as to what your situation really is.

The final document you need to work out is to truly realize how your debt is affecting you. Simply put, you need to write out the number of credit cards you have, the limits for said cards, the balances you carry, and finally the amount you pay monthly as a minimum payment against these cards. This will allow you to see in black and white how much credit card debt you have and how it's affecting you, as well as how badly it may be hitting your cash flow. You might have a bit of a rude awakening here. Be forewarned that while this may not feel good, and it may be downright depressing to examine your finances in this way, once you have done this you will know exactly where are you and where you sit. From there we can then start to examine what your journey is going to look like and where we are headed, which is freedom from debt, savings, and a good credit report!

## CALL TO ACTION

Go to www.scorebydnd.com/debttowealth and enter the code exercise2 to complete the form and download the free worksheets from our website.

# 6

# MAP

While understanding and knowing where you are is important, it is only part of the battle. Knowing you are in Toronto doesn't help you take a trip beyond understanding your starting position. You now need to determine where you want to go. What is the end destination for you? If you say to me, "I want to keep my credit report in good standing, I want to pay off my debt, AND put some money away in savings," then this book is for you! And I would say this separates you from most people and even most entrepreneurs in this world. Most are drowning in debt, and maybe have a good or decent credit report, but can't seem to keep the rating while paying down debt, let alone saving anything. Most, in fact *less than one percent*, have no real concept of what they should be trying to achieve, and certainly no idea how to go about achieving it. I'm not going to give you a specific percentage or amount in most cases as to how much you should save, or how much to reduce your debt, but I intend to give you the *process* for how to change your financial life.

Again, now that you know where you are, your next step is to decide where you want to go. Every year I decide I am going to take each of my four children on a daddy-child trip. We've been doing it since the oldest was three years old. It's rather exciting to decide where we will go, and then we sit around at home (especially as the kids get older) and figure out what we will do and where we will stay. What's important about this process is how we form a picture in our heads and then write down what our destination or end result will be. We get a real understanding of where we are going and what it looks like. So, when we get to Bruges or whatever our destination is, we already know where our hotel is, what chocolate shops we are going to visit, and even what touristy things we will do. While we are always open to changing things up when we get to our destination, we have a solid plan going into our trip.

Your destination when we're talking about your financial future is no different. You need to form a picture of exactly where you are trying to get to. Spend the time now to lay it out clearly: I want to save X% of my income a year, I want to pay off all my credit cards, and I want to keep my credit rating intact. When you can truly see it, this will help you more than having a vague idea as to what you want to do. You need to be specific, not generic, in this exercise.

In the Call to Action at the end of this chapter you can download another worksheet to assist you in doing this.

Here's a great example of this: So many people, including myself, have seen various inventions or innovations come to life and say to themselves, "Well, I had that idea five years ago," or "I had such and such an idea." In my case, as a comic book lover in my teenage years, I imagined a handheld computer where the comics would be electronic and you could have every new comic book on this thing as soon as they were released. This was before the internet, and before people were talking about digitization. It was borne out of imagination and the laziness of not wanting to house all the comics I would spend my life buying and reading. No, I didn't have a girlfriend at the time, to answer that question you might be asking. But back to my device: I didn't even know how new comics would arrive on the machine. And this thing would be light as well. Now today, this is called an iPad or tablet, and it

MAP | 31

has an app on it called comiXology, which is owned by Amazon! I may have had an idea, I may have even been somewhat specific (though in this case I would say the level of specificity was very low), but it ultimately didn't matter because I didn't execute the idea. Nor was I driven by it. I didn't form a super clear design picture and I did not do anything with it, and as a thirteen-year-old kid I'm pretty sure I wasn't able to do much if anything with it. Contrast this with the makers of the first tablet, and then Steve Jobs who created the iPad, and then the creators of ComiXology and we have this device. Why? Because they had clear pictures of what they wanted to do AND they executed their ideas.

To relate this to your debt, you need to be *specific* and have a real understanding of what it is you want to occur and then we can start to work towards achieving it. It will be a slow and arduous process, but it will also be extremely rewarding!

But I do need to ask you to count the cost of this undertaking. Please realize that this will be hard work and progress will seem slow at times, but if you can determine what it is you want, I believe you can and will absolutely achieve it. What I want you to do right now is to take a moment and write out what you want to achieve in these areas

Do you want to have savings? If so, how much? Are you willing to work hard to accomplish this goal?

Do you want to pay off your credit cards? All of them? Are you willing to change your buying habits, and at times to go without a luxury or nice-to-have item in the pursuit of your goal?

Finally, are you willing to work hard to keep your credit profile in good condition and are you willing to change your spending habits to ensure the pursuit of this goal?

If you said no to these questions, then there is no need to continue reading.

If you said maybe, I'd say keep reading, because hopefully I'll get through to you.

If you said yes, then I hope it was a "Hell yes!" And let's start moving through this process!

## CALL TO ACTION

Go to www.scorebydnd.com/debttowealth and enter the code exercise3 to complete the form and download the free worksheet from our website.

# 7

# What Do You Want to Do with Your Debt

What is it you want to see happen to your debt? Is it a function of paying off one credit card at $5,000 or is it a $50,000-in-credit-card-debt kind of situation along with other items? Whatever the case, ensure you have it written out and that you know what you want to have happen to your debt, and I hope it is *total eradication* of that debt. The bible says to write your vision down on tablets so you can run with them (Habakkuk 2:2). I'm not averse to using the Bible as a reference to help you get out of debt, so I am hoping you aren't averse to using wisdom wherever it can be found to help you succeed in achieving your goals. This bible verse was given to a prophet in Israel who was told to inform Israel that they needed to have written visions or goals in their hands so they could see them, so they could visualize them and chase them or run with them. Why? A goal unwritten and remaining only in your head is nothing more than a dream, and if you can't measure it then it really cannot be achieved.

The question remains: What do you want to do with your debt? Write out how much you have, and what you want to do it with. For example, *I want to pay off X amount of my credit card debt in 2020*. I want you to physically write down the exact amount you wish to pay off.

In the Call to Action at the end of this chapter you can download another worksheet to assist you in doing this.

If we use me as an example, there was a time in my life when I needed to pay off almost $100,000 in credit card debt! It was absolutely insane. I had foolishly used the money to cover some purchases for the business and I did not pull the money back out of the company and suddenly found myself in some massive debt. I was not thrilled about it and I knew I needed to pay it down. What was I going to do?

Well, the first thing I did (and I kid you not) was exactly what I have shown you here, I needed to assess where I actually was. How much debt did I have, what was I spending my money on, what shape was my credit report in (this is pretty important, and we'll unpack it later). I even took a good look at my net worth. I learned a few things by doing this. I was cash poor and asset rich, which was why my cards were on the rise and not the decline. I also learned I had made some, a few, smart choices. Although I had the habit of saving, unfortunately I also had the habit of spending. It's a true statement my mom always told me: *A fool and his money will always be easily parted*. Well, I was surely being parted from it as I was putting it in foolish areas, along with a few smart areas.

Once I had written down on paper and looked at how much debt I had AND I looked at the fact that some of my credit card statements clearly stated that if I paid only the minimum balance every month, it would take well over 100 years to pay off my debt, then I had a very sobering and rude awakening to what was happening to me. I realized something, and I hope you do too when you look at your expenses: I was enjoying a *lot* of different things and I needed to change my habits and limit how I spent. The position I was in, however, was exacerbated by having access to a *lot* of credit, which meant I needed to work extra hard to change my behaviors and pay off my debt.

My point here is that you must clearly define your goal for what you are hoping to accomplish. Physically write it out!

At this point, you have or should have assessed exactly where you are, and you know where you want to go, but how do you get there? How do you go from knowing you have a lot of debt and knowing you want to pay it off to actually making it happen?

That's what we are going to come to shortly. But first, like the bible tells kings when they are thinking about going to war, we need to count the cost. I promise you two things: First, this isn't going to be easy, in fact it may be very painful. But second, it will also be extremely rewarding.

## CALL TO ACTION

Go to www.scorebydnd.com/debttowealth and enter the code exercise4 to complete the form and download the free worksheet from our website.

# 8

# It's Not Going to Make Sense

The first thing I am going to tell you to do, and it won't make sense, is to get a *charge card*, no matter how many credit cards you already have in your wallet and no matter what your debt level is, this is going to become your best friend. Every card company has a charge card. A charge card has two really key benefits we are going to focus on. Firstly, as a part of the credit network, you can use them anywhere and secondly, because it's a charge card you absolutely cannot not carry a balance at the end of the month. This is not a credit card, it's a monthly loan account, and the loan is due monthly.

With a few simple steps and using this type of card, you can move from carrying a balance on your cards to never carrying a balance and still have the ability to do the following: 1) keep your credit rating in good standing; 2) save money; 3) track your spending; and 4) use it wherever credit cards are accepted. And while I know it's not going to make sense, but unless you have wild discipline or are extremely wealthy, *eliminate cash from your life*. When you carry cash, you feel a kind of "high" every time you see it in your wallet, and you are more likely to spend that money. Cash bleeds out of your wallet or purse faster than you can imagine! If you insist on carrying cash, carry an extremely small amount and write out exactly where each penny, and I mean *every* penny, goes. Make it extremely difficult to use cash.

Now, some of you will say, "But Bill, I like to buy a cola or a coffee every day and I need cash for that." My humble opinion is you should stop buying that stuff because it'll kill you. But if you have to buy it, buy in bulk for home and not from Starbucks every morning because those fancy coffee beverages are just stupidly expensive. Remember, you won't succeed without making some changes. $1 a day for a year, such as 365 colas, could be one or two card payments or even a car payment. My point here is that you will need to make some changes, and I'll walk you through those changes, but you have to be willing to do it!

## CALL TO ACTION

Go to www.scorebydnd.com and review our Score by DND card to learn more about charge cards. Our charge card is a non-debt product, unlike the majority of credit card products available in the marketplace.

# 9

# A Short Story

You will have to give up something (or many somethings) to succeed. What is your reaction to that statement? "But I don't want to give anything up!" Yeah, neither did I, but that just isn't realistic. Let me tell you a story to illustrate:

When I was in my late twenties and started saving for a house, I recognized three things that would happen with each paycheck I received: 1) I would make a donation or tithe to my church, 2) I then immediately set aside some savings, which went into multiple areas where I had no chance of touching the money (we're going to talk about this principle later), and then 3) everything else was spent. I wasn't too worried about this because I was in a place in my life where I was saving for the future, I had a few credit cards that were always paid off, and it was important to me to do charitable giving. Beyond that I was more than happy to spend and spend and spend!

I may have had a leg up on many people because my wallet had four cards in it. One corporate credit card that was always paid off for small corporate purchases as needed, one personal credit card with a sizeable limit for the rare times I needed to carry a balance and/or my American Express card was not accepted, an American Express charge card (the single greatest credit device to me in the world and I'll explain that later), and an emergency card that was kept tucked away in the house away from me in the off chance some massive emergency occurred and I needed to do something about it. It took me the better part of my twenties to get to this point, but I was there before I got married at age twenty-six. Now, don't get too annoyed that I started off better than perhaps your situation because I'll explain later how much worse off I was before and what I did to fix that as well. I give you these details so you understand how I had credit available to me, but I was not saving for a house yet and I wanted to. And I spent like crazy.

What do I mean by that? On my Amex I could spend some obscene amounts, this was well before the credit crisis, so to spend on new clothing, or a watch, or a vacation in a month was never really a big deal to me. If it was a really big purchase, I'd have the retailer chunk out the payments over the year (this is how I paid for my vacation every year). It was amazing how accommodating people were if you were spending like crazy.

Here is the issue: I knew I had to pay off my American Express at the end of the month every single month, there was no leeway in holding a balance. So I had a good idea as to what I could or could not spend over the course of the month. Now, it's important to understand, it's not how much you can spend, it's the fact that you *do* spend, and for me it was significant. So I did something either smart or stupid, but considering it helped me save enough to put a thirty-percent down payment on my home (it wasn't the only thing, but it was the main habit piece for me), I think it worked very well.

What did I do? I moved *everything* to my charge card. What do I mean by that? I knew I had X as a payment ability every month, but having money come out of my bank and my card and then trying to save up for a mortgage was proving too difficult. So, the first thing I did was move every single purchase to my charge card. I did this for four reasons:

1) if I had an upper limit as to what I could spend, and I knew how much I could spend a month, then by pre-spending an amount every month I wasn't going to feel the loss of what I was spending on. Let me explain this in more detail and I'll use some outlandish numbers so it really hits home. If I was spending $5,000 a month on clothing, and I had $1,000 a month in must-have costs that could be moved to my charge card, which had to be paid off at the end of the month, then I would move my cell phone, my cable bill, and other small costs over to the card. If these netted out to $1,000 a month, then I was simply left with $4,000 to be able to spend on my card for clothing. I would in essence have all my purchases itemized on one statement, I knew exactly what was being spent and I knew the max I could spend.

2) I removed cash from my life wherever it was at all possible to do so. I don't know about you, but when I have a ton of cash I feel flush, and that old saying of a fool and his money are soon parted inevitably comes to pass. So every single purchase went to the American Express charge card. Now what if it's a small purchase like $2 for a donut and coffee? I simply gave it up. And it was easy because I couldn't just whip out cash to pay for it. Instead, I had to think to myself whether I should charge such a small amount to my card. If you have really good discipline, you will spend less this way, simply because you don't want to reach into your pocket to pull out your card to make a purchase for such a small amount. If you want to really curb the urge to spend on small items, keep a written journal of every single purchase you make. When you physically know you have to write it out every time you spend, you will simply be too lazy to buy the item. It's easier to keep the money in your "wallet." The big question here many people have is what if people don't accept American Express, or only

want cash? I'll be honest, and this is just me, but in those cases I simply didn't buy the item. Now, I don't want to sound like I'm an AmEx commercial, because both Visa and MasterCard also offer charge cards. It doesn't matter which one you favor. For me, American Express was a very good choice *because* it's not taken everywhere.

3) I asked my church to accept my charge card because this way everything was hitting my card for the reasons I've mentioned to you (tracking all expenses in one place). My church found a way to accept card payments pretty easily and found I wasn't the only one who wanted to be able to give by card. Today this is pretty common.

4) And for me this was the kicker, I even charged my house savings to the charge card, which was a little tricky to do. I had a friend who had a credit card terminal, so I asked him to run my card on my new card day (the day when you have a new card statement) for the amount I wanted to save each month for a house. This friend took whatever service fees were required and then gave me a check for the amount, which I then deposited into a separate bank account and started building up a balance for my future mortgage. Now you may ask why would I do that? It's costing me interest and fees and I still have to pay it off at the end of the month. Well, let me explain. Firstly, I didn't pay interest on the charge card because it wasn't considered a cash advance and I had to pay it off at month's end, so there was no interest. While I did have to pay the fees for my friend's cost to run my card, this gave me something far more important, which was reducing the balance I had left that could be spent monthly. In short, it forced me to save, and it did wonders for me. I saved a massive amount towards my home in a relatively short period of time because it was all my unnecessary purchases that were being eliminated.

But I asked *you* what are *you* willing to give up? Let's recap. I had a charge card already, so I moved all my monthly payments I could move onto the card, including my church donations. I eliminated cash out of my life as much as I could. These things had a compound effect because I could only spend  a set amount on a charge card that would force me to pay it off at the end of the month. I was effectively reducing my frivolous spending by pre-using my limit. I was also moving my important spends onto the card to reduce the potential tension of not being able to pay them because of spending from multiple sources. Finally, I also created a forced savings routine through this card, which allowed me to save money from the top of my card spending limit as opposed to waiting until the end of the month to see what might be left over. Here is a critical tip: There is nothing left over at the end of the month, ever! My method forced me to curb my spending.

Maybe you're saying to yourself, "But Bill, I'm already at my limits. I can't physically save in this fashion, or if I move things to my card then I won't have enough for X, Y, or Z." I'm glad you brought that up because it's the topic of the next chapter!

# 10

# What are You Willing to Give Up?

Here is where the rubber starts to hit the road. If you agree to move all your costs to your charge card, and if you're willing to go to forced savings, but your hard reality is that there is more month than money, how do you make this work? The answer is really, really carefully.

Remember that list of payments that go out of your account monthly (the cable, the internet, and so on)? Which of those payments are you *willing to give up*? And what amount does that add up to? I really mean it! If I told you that if you cut cable and dropped your internet down to the slowest speed offered instead of the fastest, and you and I both know you have that one-gigabyte internet circuit, you can probably live with that. What else do you pay for that you really don't need? Do you have two cell phones and a landline? Can anything there be cut? How much can you cut that is really just a waste? Can you move from Starbucks at $5 a coffee to making it at home which only cost you something like thirty cents? You need to truly consider what you can stop spending on and write down that total number.

As you might be able to guess, we have a download to assist you. You'll find it in the Call to Action below.

Good things come from sacrifice, so listen to me when I tell you this: If you will really follow what I am laying out here in this book, you *will* reduce your debt, and if you can get excited about that then you *will* succeed. And if you need that dopamine hit of spending, well I'm going to show you how to *spend yourself out of debt*—which makes no sense, but it works, trust me!

So right now is when you have to really decide what you are willing to give up and write that down.

## CALL TO ACTION

Go to www.scorebydnd.com/debttowealth and enter the code exercise5 to complete the form and download the free worksheet from our website.

# 11

# How Do We Get to NYC?

Now you have a few things you understand: You have an understanding of where you are, you know where you want to go, you have brought your key resource to this journey (the charge card), and you have determined what you are willing to give up. Now the questions is this: How do you start moving towards your destination?

If you don't have a charge card yet, go to the Call to Action at the end of this chapter to learn about the Score Card by DND.

The goal in this beginning phase is to have every single purchase wherever possible be either a direct withdrawal out of your account (mortgage or rent payment, insurance, etc.), and the balance needs to go on your charge card. The card spending will give you a dopamine hit when you spend on it. How do I know this? Because you have credit card debt! You should also be able to make an arrangement such that the day after you get paid is when your card is due. Why? Because that way you aren't tempted to put the money anywhere else. And knowing that your regular bills are coming off this one card, which you pay religiously and completely pay off, means you shouldn't start going backwards, unless you are overspending. And if you're overspending then you need to truly drop some costs.

However, I haven't addressed the big kicker, which is this: How do you actually pay off our credit card debt? I'm so glad you asked! You need to realize a couple of things. The principles I have taught you (the way to spend and curb your spending is to set up what I call "pre-spending") means you likely won't notice the loss of the money, especially when you start saving. The reason why is because you will be putting the same amount on your charge card every month, and if your pre-spending includes savings, you will simply spend less on unneeded items.

So how do you pay down your credit cards? I'll walk you through an example I personally went through when I was in my early twenties.

As you and I both know, paying off credit card debt beyond the minimum payments is pretty difficult. I understand that, so I am going to now show you how to do it. Here are the tools you will need: 1) your credit card statements and 2) the amount you are willing to give up. My assumption is that you are able to make your minimum payments already on your cards, including any over-limit fees or other penalties.

I need you to line up your statements from the lowest-balance most-maxed card to the highest balance card. You need to add up your minimum payments (including whatever the overage fees are as most likely at least one of your cards is maxed, which is why you have multiple cards).

In the Call to Action at the end of this chapter, you will be directed to a handy worksheet that will assist you with this.

Here is what you are going to do.

**Step 1:** Pay each card's minimum payment.

**Step 2:** From the higher-balance cards, you will take out as close as you possibly can via cash advance the amount you just paid. But this DOES NOT mean go further in debt if the card is not maxed! It means if you had a $200 minimum payment and you are able to take out $150 from the card as a cash advance, then you do it. But the key here is *do not increase your debt amount*.

**Step 3:** Depending on how many cards you have, this is where the acceleration factor will have a massive effect. You take all the funds cash-advanced from the higher-balance cards, PLUS the minimum payment for the lowest-balance card PLUS the amount of money you have "saved" from giving up the wasted purchases, and you smack all of that hard against the lowest-balance card. This is the key strategy for paying off credit card debt. And now and I will share that personal example I told you about.

For me, I was already making my minimum payment but felt like I was spinning my wheels. I decided I could do with cutting about $200 of my expenses at the time, so it wasn't a lot, and I had several cards, more than I care to admit, but at the time there were Visa cards from two banks, a Diners Club Card, an AmEx, a store card, and a Mastercard. In my case, the store card had the lowest balance, so that was the one I was going after first. I paid all the minimum payments on the two Visa cards, let's say it was $200 each, plus Diners Club ($100) plus Mastercard ($100) and then I withdrew those same amounts from an ATM, giving me $400. My store card had a minimum payment of $100 a month, and then I had a $200 amount I had saved from cutting expenses. This gave me a gross amount of $700 in cash and I put it all against the store card. At the time, the store card total balance was $2,500 and was maxed out.

I want to make two key points here: I had firstly paid all my credit cards (minimum payments only) so I had fulfilled my card holder obligation, and then took out cash advances from each one. Secondly, instead of taking well over two years (especially when you factor in interest on a maxed 25% store card) to pay down the store card, I made the pay off period just four months! I paid $700 a month over four months for a grand total of $2,800 (the extra $300 was a good approximation of the interest I would pay). And I did it by leveraging my other credit cards (the cash advances) without adding to the overall level of credit card debt I was carrying.

At the end of the fourth month I celebrated with something small, and we'll talk about goal-setting and celebrating victories later because it's extremely important! And then I put the card away. And if you need to, put it under lock and key! The important thing *is I did not cut it up*, and *I did not cancel it*. Why not? Because you want to protect your credit rating, and for the time being you want to show you are responsible with your credit cards, including store cards. You also don't want to suddenly drop the amount you have access to as that hits your credit rating hard. There is a way to get rid of credit cards without damaging your credit rating, *but not when you are in the process of paying them down*. So if this is you, put it in a block of ice if you don't trust yourself, but do not cancel it. It's no good to teach you how to get out of debt if you don't also learn good spending habits and discipline.

Back to my example. In month five I still had $700 to put against credit card debt. It is extremely important you do NOT reduce this amount that you have available to put towards your credit card debt each month. I had gotten along just fine without that money, and I still had plenty of credit card debt I wanted to eliminate using the same method. If the next card was one with a $4,000 balance, then I started hitting that one with this $700 a month. And in six or seven months (because of interest charges), that card was paid off.

The really great thing is you are hitting the principal balance owed by large amounts every month. You are also focusing on the lowest-balance cards first because they will be faster to pay off, which gives you early victories and momentum to take on the next card. It's also really important to note that unless you have a credit card at 50% interest, I will keep telling you to pay off cards based on the balance owed from lowest to highest, not based on which ones have the highest interest rates.

Also, to address the elephant in the room, yes you are being hit with cash-advance fees, but most cash-advance fees will be in the range of three to five percent higher than purchase interest. This is simply a cost to paying down your debt, and you mustn't let your fear of a little bit of interest stop you from actually making a major dent in your debt. This is one of the key factors people don't tell you about interest: You simply have to pay it sometimes. Period. Don't get hung up about paying another three percent in interest charges if you are able to pay off a two-year debt (or two hundred year debt the way the system is structured against you) in just four months! The win is in the accelerated payments to the point the interest charge really doesn't matter.

This, my friends, is how you get to New York City. In my example, I believe it took me just over two-and-a-half years to pay off six cards. I was saving and I was paying down my debt and keeping my credit rating high. If you take nothing else out of this book, please realize that this one key strategy not *might* but *WILL* get you out of credit card debt. I've used it with lines of credit as well. This is the power of accelerated payment, and it's far more important than any short-term interest you get charged.

Here's a recap since this is so important:

1. Take an amount you can reduce from your expenses. Any amount is fine as this is just going to help you pay off your debt faster, but the higher the better, obviously.
2. Figure out which card has the lowest balance, ignore the others for now, and make this card your enemy.
3. Pay all your minimum payments on other cards first, then pull off via cash advance that exact amount or as close to it (less interest charges) as you can get without increasing your balance and pay down the card noted in step two until you pay it off.
4. Once paid off, lock it away but do not cancel it because you need to protect your credit rating.
5. Rinse and repeat with the next lowest-balance card!

This process will take you years to accomplish depending on how much debt you have. However, it will be *so rewarding* to get out from under it. Further, and it goes without saying, do not spend on these cards! That's why you have your charge card, and you should be using it for all your regular purchases.

But all this begs the question: Why do we even need credit or a good credit rating? And that will be what I tackle in the next chapter.

## CALL TO ACTION

Go to www.scorebydnd.com to learn and potentially apply for the Score card by DND or contact us at the website and we'll be happy to discuss the merits of our cards vs the competition.

Go to www.scorebydnd.com/debttowealth and enter the code exercise6 to complete the form and download the free worksheet from our website.

# 12

# Why Do We Need a Good Credit Score Today?

Frankly it's the world we are living in. If you are self-employed, a business owner, an entrepreneur, or simply most people in the West, a valid and strong credit rating is extremely important. I'll give you a few examples as to why.

When you want to get a cell phone under contract your credit report is checked. When you open up a bank account your credit report is checked. If you are applying to open an account with any kind of business, whether it's an accounting firm, a legal firm, or even for utilities such as water, typically your personal or your corporate credit is checked. This is not to mention when you actually want money from a bank or credit card company. And some jobs, depending on the level of seniority in the company, require a credit check. And even when you look to rent a home or office space, your credit report is checked. Bad credit essentially locks you out of having a better life; it excludes you from being able to step up into a better quality of life.

In all of these cases your credit report is reviewed. In some cases it may just be your corporate credit report, but in all cases when you look to do business with someone in any area, they are looking at your credit report to some degree. Think of it as your resumé when you're looking to get a job.

You might say, "I didn't give permission to the law firm to check my credit," and you might be right; you may have only given them the okay to check you out corporately, for which they don't need your permission, but they will check you out personally as well. This is why we put credit references or trade references on applications to start with a new company. I'll bet you dollars to donuts that one of the companies you set up as your reference, and whom you typically have terms with and a good rapport, have checked your credit. So, when your lawyer calls them, it takes only a few questions to see if you are worthy from a credit standpoint or not.

Your credit report is very much like a financial resumé to people. While we'll dissect it a little later, it's important to understand that any relationships in the business world are looking to check this out. So, if it's bad or poor it will make life tougher for you, not easier. Just like you may put a lot of effort into protecting your employment resumé, such as trying not to jump from position to position every year, it's also extremely important to protect your credit report. The hard thing is you may not know what your credit report says unless you actually pull it. It may be painful to look at as well. That's okay because I'll walk you through how to correct and protect it going forward.

I want to really emphasize that the difference between this book and most other books I've seen that talk about how to get out of debt, is how most don't touch the credit bureau side of things. I think it's extremely important to not just understand what it means to have credit, but also good credit and how to keep it that way, or repair it if need be.

I also want to impress upon you that your credit rating and the need for credit far surpasses just asking for money or loans. Typically, everywhere we go our credit is being looked at, and how we treat it will determine how other businesses treat us. To bring it home to you, when you set up your utilities at home, if you're being asked for a deposit, it's typically because you have a weaker credit rating and they feel it's going to be a bit of work to collect payments from you. If your bank puts a hold on your deposits for five days (or more), then I'm sorry to say you have a lower than desired credit score. Good credit is the difference between required deposits on car leases and whether you are asked for retainers ahead of time.

I hope I have given you enough reasons why you want to have good credit.

The second part of this discussion of why we need credit today is equally important. Credit is the amount of someone else's money you can make use of, and hopefully to your advantage and not your detriment. If you have no credit at all, the other side of most financial transactions such as the ones I mentioned above, will have a certain distrust for you because there is no history of how you pay your bills, there is no track record of your payment profile over time. Thus, there is no way to gauge what kind of person you are when it comes to paying back your commitments. Credit is therefore needed so you can actually create a profile of how you pay, which in turn will allow you to set up accounts with your mobile phone, your utilities, and even rent a place without too much hassle. Not having credit, or having weak credit, will usually ensure higher deposits in these realms. Good credit will broaden your abilities to not just borrow, but also who will do business with you, who will work with you, and what you can actually access on a service basis.

# 13

# What Do We Look at When Looking at Credit?

Let's break down then what is actually in your credit report. This will vary by company (credit bureau) and country, but there are a several essentials common to most credit reports.

First is the identifying information. Your name, date of birth, any alternate names you may have used, your address, and previous addresses, and sometimes your spouse. It's important to understand this is to ensure that the correct report is being allocated to you. For example, my son and I live in the same home, and he is only seven at the time of this writing. However, our credit report will show both of our names as Kamran Dost, and it will show us at the same home, and the same previous address. How does an analyst confirm they are looking at the right person, besides the fact that my son doesn't yet have a credit footprint. Firstly, our middle names would be in the other names used section, mine being Bill and his being Christian. Secondly, our dates of birth would show me in my forties and my son under the age of ten. It would also show a spouse attached to me. A person reviewing this could determine who is the correct Kamran they want to review.

The next section usually has a number, which is your overall credit score. This is typically somewhere between 300-900, depending on the company doing the score and the country, so in Canada the highest score is 900. In the USA using a FICO score model the highest score is 850, but FICO's competitor goes up to 900. It's beyond the scope of this discussion to go into the different scoring systems, or what numbers are the highest. In fact, it really doesn't matter. What does matter is that regardless of company and country you are typically looking for a score between 650-700 or higher. Below 600 and in fact below 650 typically means you have a weaker credit history, and over 650 or into the higher numbers typically means you have a better credit rating. Your goal, though, should be to break into the 700 and above range. The UK is slightly different with its credit agencies being a little more varied, but the mid-600s rule generally holds true as does the goal of wanting to break into the 700s. To pinpoint this, each agency does have the number that's considered as "good" on their website.

This number is the sum of all the different factors in your credit report that I will discuss here. What you want to focus on is keeping this number higher by doing and having the right behaviors. The number isn't the focus, the behaviors are, because good behaviors will lead to a better score. I personally suggest you look to purchase a credit report service under the free trial, download the report and then cancel the service. There is no need to spend unnecessary money on a monthly basis right now, however the free trial may force a month of cost on you, though I'm not sure how that is free! And it will give you a baseline on your report. Besides your score, called a beacon, will be a few sentences as to why your credit score is where it is. Often it says some pretty unhelpful things such as, accounts in service too high, delinquency, accounts too new or possible judgements, and so on, but these are generic markers and are not indicative of your credit. You need to realize that it's just meant to be a quick gauge as to where you are. Today you may find some credit cards and banks are giving you access to your report, but these are not as accurate as a direct report from the credit agency or bureau itself. However, you only need a quick gauge, and free is always better when we are trying to save. I suggest you look at downloading your score every ninety days

Go to the Call to Action at the end of this chapter to get a helpful worksheet.

The next section of your report will have any collection actions, court judgements, or liens against you (both good and bad liens). If a collection agency is calling you, it will be listed here, if your cellphone company got a judgement against you it will be here, and if you have a car lease there will be a lien showing here that states someone else has an interest in some of your assets.

The next part of the report is the most important, it is your actual payment history. EVERY piece of credit you have or have had—that store card at Ikea, that Visa you forgot about from when you were in university, your student loan, and your mortgage—are all noted here, along with the following information;

1. The last time this company, such as Visa reported on your report, typically monthly.
2. The highest credit allowed against such account.
3. The amount you have borrowed against the highest credit. This includes if you are over the limit.
4. What your monthly payment is supposed to be.
5. How you pay, showing a history up to a few years on your payment profile, if you pay late, and how many months late.

6. There is a notes section for a creditor to repot, such as judgement being sought, or account closed at creditor's request, account closed at bank's request, and so on.

7. The individual company typically has a rating against you that will show if this is a monthly payment, a variable payment, an instalment payment, and how you pay them. The higher the number the worse the score. So, an R for revolving credit with a 1 means you pay on time. An R2 would mean you're currently 30 days late, and so on. and R9 means the amount was written off.

For us, here is what is important, everyone you borrow from is on here and how you pay them back is also listed, when you are late they tell on you and if you are over the limit this is also noted.

The next section is how many inquiries have been made on your report. As a rule, creditors know your credit needs to be reviewed, but too many inquiries is a bad thing and makes it look like you are credit seeking. Typically, if you have a couple of checks every six months you'll be okay. However, beware if, for example, you switch banks and you look to open up commercial and personal accounts and also pick up a couple of credit cards and maybe a line of credit. Depending on the institution, your credit will be checked multiple times. This will have a negative effect on your credit rating. When I switched banks, I went to two banks to get a look at what was out there, and between them they hit my report six times in thirty days, which created a red flag on my credit report. Expect the same to happen to you. Also note that most ongoing credit services are given permission to check your credit every year. It is written into their contract and as a client you would have signed off on this, whether you were aware or not. The same thing happens from Visa, American express, Mastercard, and so on. they want to know where you are on at least an annual basis. Some of these companies are able to do this on what is called a "soft" basis, such as those that provide you a charge card with no pre-set spending limit. A soft hit means that it won't show up on your report, while others can only make a hard hit against your credit report when checking it. Just be aware you have provided these companies the permission to check your credit on an ongoing basis.

When reviewing your credit, a company will first confirm it's you, then check to see if you are stable where you are living. Do you have any major negatives via collections or judgements? How many open accounts do you have and how do you pay them? Are any of them over the limit? What about how long you have had these accounts? And how often are you seeking credit. Once this is reviewed, an analyst will also look at your beacon score to see how you compare against other people they lend to and against the averages in the country.

While it's more of an art then a science, some companies have hard and fast rules, such as a low beacon score will mean NO on your loan application, as might other red flags such as a judgement against you. Beyond this they may even have their own internal system that does a special analysis to either approve or decline you based on other factors called a modeling system.

There are also a few indicators on the report. If you have used up more than 85% of your available credit, you are considered "maxed out" and most companies will typically not look to offer you more credit. The jump from 85% to 100% in borrowing is such a short leap that lenders assume if you are at 85% of borrowing you are essentially at 100%. So, it's always important to keep your credit card accounts, which are considered revolving accounts, at under 85% capacity at first. However, you'll be much better off by keeping them under 35%. Why? Because 35% or below means you are using a very low amount of credit and can be trusted with more, or at least with what you have.

Having four credit cards all above 85% would indicate a warning to most creditors. As we discussed how to pay off your credit cards, it's important to understand why I said to keep the credit card once it's paid off. If you have four cards with a total allowable credit of $20,000 and all four are maxed out, then this is a bad thing. But when you pay off one card completely (say it was $5,000), you now have $15,000 used of $20,000 available. While the individual cards are still maxed except one, which is still a bad thing, your overall utilization of credit facilities is at 75% of total credit allowed. This is a good thing! When you pay off the second card at $5,000, you now still have two maxed out cards, bad, but you have an overall usage of 50%, good. And this will start to affect your credit rating in a positive way. It shows you can hold credit facilities and maybe you just use two cards a lot, or had run them up but were working on it.

Companies performing a manual review will see this and see that things aren't necessarily as bad as your score may show. This is the chief reason I have stated you need to keep the accounts open. Once you have paid off your cards, you can then determine what you should or should not cancel, but you'll do it from a position of strength and knowledge, showing you have balances available to you and you have paid others down or off and this will help improve your credit. After eliminating all your credit card debt, that's when you can cancel one or two cards without them causing a negative hit on your credit report.

## CALL TO ACTION

Go to www.scorebydnd.com/debttowealth and enter the code exercise7 to complete the form and download the free worksheet from our website.

# 14

# Unravelling Your Personal Credit Report

Hopefully at this point you have pulled out your credit report to take a good look at it. I encourage you to work through it and see where you may personally feel your credit is at. Is it good? Is it bad? Do you have work to do? And do you understand what you need to do? As I don't know your personal situation and I am not a credit counsellor, I always advise that if you can't understand something, or need more clarification for your specific situation or country, please speak to a professional. This book does not take your personal situation into consideration and is not meant to serve as a replacement for the expertise of a professional credit counselling professional.

I say this for two reasons: Yes, it's a bit of a disclaimer that I am not taking responsibility if you do something that really harms your livelihood. But more importantly, I do actually care about you as fellow human being, and there's only so much I can give you from my own personal experiences and observations in a book. If you feel your situation is unique then it is likely you need to seek out someone who can look at your personal circumstances and assist you. I'm not there to do that and I'd never want you to turn around and say "I read this book and figured it was one-size-fits-all but then I ran into troubles." Be smart, and when in doubt please seek professional assistance.

## CALL TO ACTION

Go to www.scorebydnd.com/debttowealth and refer to our database of resources that can assist you in finding the help you may need. If we don't provide the kind of help you need, we can likely point you in the right direction!

# 15

# How Can You Correct Something You Just Don't Understand?

It is extremely important, just as it is with your net worth statement and your statement of incoming and outgoing money, that you truly understand your credit report. I want to really encourage you as I did earlier to pull a copy of your credit report and learn how to fully understand it. Read what it says and absorb it.

Is everything correct? Did you live at the addresses noted? Did you actually not pay that mobile phone bill on time? Or was your credit card payment late? Is there anything on there that shouldn't be there? If everything is accurate that's great because then you can focus on the items that are causing you problems. You want to isolate them so you can understand your report. If there is a problem with accuracy, every bureau by law gives you a way to dispute these issues and you need to follow the guidance on their websites.

Items that affect your report negatively include the following:

1.  Too many inquiries on your credit report—it makes you look like you are seeking credit or debt and if you

are being checked often this will reduce your credit score.

2.  Any collection actions or judgements against you will show up and will typically stay on your credit report until you pay things off (longer in the case of bankruptcy).

3.  When you look at your individual accounts, be aware that every time you are late or are over your credit limits on your cards WILL affect you negatively. Also, whenever you have more than 85% utilization of your credit accounts will negatively impact your report. Few realize that if they simply paid their bills on time and kept under their max balances by a reasonable amount, their credit rating would increase. These are simple and effective actions you can take.

4.  Unfortunately, if you move a lot it is interpreted as a tendency towards instability, so you need to ensure you aren't moving every year. The big issue about moving is that if a lender sees you move around a lot, they fear if you become delinquent then they won't know where to find you.

Furthermore, just because you think you have good credit doesn't mean you to. What do I mean by this? You could be doing the "right" things but still have poor credit. How is this possible? If your cards are maxed out, and your payments only cover the minimum amount due, and you have just opened a new credit account, you could end up with a very low credit score! If you add in a couple of late payments then this can really skew your credit score down. Just because you have a $20,000 limit doesn't mean your card should be maxed out to that level!

So please be aware of the fact that paying monthly and on time won't necessarily give you a "good" credit score. It's not difficult to keep up a good rating. It's about changing habits, one of them being do not keep your cards maxed, even if you are paying them down.

# 16

# When Do I Start Cancelling Cards and Lines?

This is a very good question and I'm glad you asked it. One of the items on your credit report talks about your credit utilization, and while it is true that too many lines and access to too much credit can harm your credit report, it's far worse to always look like you are maxed out as opposed to the impression you have a lot of credit available to you and aren't using a lot of it.

What I mean by this is the following: If you have $20,000 in credit card debt spread over four credit cards and then pay off two of them, you should keep those cards open, in fact you need to. You need to either put the card with a trusted friend, or inside an ice block, or even in a safety deposit box if you don't trust yourself, but you need to keep the line open. Why? Because your credit report will look more favorable if you have $10,000 of $20,000 of your available credit utilized (even if half of the cards are maxed) as opposed to having all $10,000 of available credit being maxed out because you cancelled the other two cards after paying them off. You will have hurt yourself, not helped. Please be aware, if you really need to cancel any debt instruments, the time to do it is when *all* them have been paid off. In this way you can arguably show that 1) you can handle larger amounts of debt and 2) you made a conscious decision to reduce your credit availability from a position of strength by having all the debt paid off, as opposed to reducing your debt limit and still looking like you are maxed out.

I'm not going to go into what happens if there are emergencies and so forth as I still prefer you don't max yourself out even if there is an emergency, but I will show you how to plan for that in the future. Please note that this entire section is based on you not spending more money than you currently are spending. You'll recall you cut some costs to get a base line of money you could spend on paying down debt, and then you added to it by simply taking the payments you were currently making on debt and simply accelerating the pay-down of your cards by focusing on one card at a time. It will cost you some cash advance interest, but the effect of paying down your credit cards will prevent you from paying *massive* amounts of interest down the road when you're on the slow-boat of just paying minimum amounts due. It's really important to acknowledge that at this point you haven't spent any more money than you were previously spending—you've simply shifted what that money is going to, which is paying down debt instead of other things you don't really need. This means that anyone and everyone can do this to pay off their credit cards.

I hope this realization gets you excited, because you aren't spending any less than you were spending before, which means you are in fact "spending yourself to debt freedom!"

Finally, I also want to remind you of something: You now have a charge card, which will only allow you to spend what you can pay off at the end of the month, you will have to remember that every time you spend on this card it *must be paid off at the end of the month*. In this way you are aren't going to dig yourself into an even deeper hole. The next step we'll get to is to learning how to actually save some money.

## CALL TO ACTION

Have you gone to www.scorebydnd.com and signed up for our free blog? Or have you emailed us at debttowealth@scorebydnd.com for free resources to go along with this book? Do it now! Also, you can apply for the DND charge card at www.scorebydnd.com and we can walk you through this process with the kind of card we've been explaining to you all along. Our video is here at www.scorebydnd.com and I suggest you start there to get more information.

# Part II

## Debt

# 17

# Why Get Out of Debt?

It's a simple question with a not-so-simple answer. Most would say, "So I won't have to pay interest, but not all debt and not all interest is a bad thing." It's a bad thing, however, when you are paying more interest month after month and have no hope of getting out of debt.

For the purposes of this book there are really only two kinds of debt.

The first is your mortgage or a loan for anything that has a regular or fixed payment amount, so an investment, a car loan (or lease as it may be), these are considered for the time being as "good debt."

Then there is bad debt—this is the debt that gets you in trouble. It includes the credit cards or lines of credit that have no normal pay down (or amortization) of the borrowed amounts. Bad debts are bad because you don't have a built-in plan to pay it off, or It's getting really complicated when you attempt to do so. This is the kind of debt you want to pay off as much as possible as we discussed earlier, and you were losing a fair amount of money because of the interest being charged.

These don't have to have high interest rates either. A line of credit typically has a very low rate of interest, but if you don't handle it correctly it can be a very bad form of debt. Today, banks are offering home equity lines of credit tied to your shrinking mortgage. In essence, as you pay your mortgage down and there is equity built up in your home, a line of credit runs alongside it, offering you more and more money. You are basically removing the equity out of your home. In small cases there is some really good value to this, but if you are not paying off this debt, only paying the interest on it, this means you are never actually paying your home off, you're simply moving the equity into the line of credit and then spending it. While there are times and places that this can be a good thing, in general I would say it's not a good idea. You must have extreme discipline to not spend up your home into things you can't see.

Finally, an area of debt I'm not really going to cover is business debt, such as lines of credit, loans, and leases to help you grow your business. These all have a place and a purpose, but it's not the point of this book to delve too far into this except to note that anything that helps you grow your business can be seen as good and anything that's not providing you a return on your debt is likely a bad debt. In other words, if you are using a line of credit to pay suppliers who then allow you to sell to customers and then pay them off, this is a good debt. But if it's simply to pay your bills, then you need to look at your company and determine what you need to do to fix it!

# 18

# Do You Want More Money in Your Bank Account?

Of course you want more money in your bank account, right? Well, paying off your debt over time will do this for you. I bring this to your attention because it's hard work to pay off debt, and while you are paying down your debt it will feel like you have less money, but this is because you're only going to be spending money you have on your charge card and you'll be limiting your spending ability. However, after taking that bitter pill for a short period of time, you will find you do have more money in your bank account. This is because you will stop paying interest once you pay down this debt. Further, as we'll discuss, you will learn to live within your means, which really means *below* your means, because once that debt is paid off you will have a pretty fantastic opportunity to make some really positive long-term decisions.

What do I mean by this? This book has three basic points to it:

1. Learn to pay off your debt.
2. Keep your credit report in good condition while you pay down that debt.
3. Learn to save money.

I've explained the reasons why you should pay off your debt, and I've taken you through the steps of how to do so. I've also explained why you want to keep your credit report in good condition while you pay down your debt and how to go about doing that. As we start to move into the next topics, I really want to ensure you agree with these principles. Next up is why you should bother saving money.

# 19

# Why Save and How Do I Get to that Mindset?

I previously mentioned how more than 16 million adults in the UK have less than £100 in savings, and that one out of every four households has less than £95 in savings! I find this extremely frightening, and I hope you do too. Savings are important for a myriad of reasons. First, if something happens that was just not planned, you need to have savings, such as an emergency car repair or a surprise home repair. These are very real challenges, and you need to ensure you have savings in order to address them. The temptation to use your credit cards during these "emergencies" can be very tempting, but that could put you back in that debt situation again. By learning to save—truly save—you will have funds for such an emergency. In 2008, the world entered a credit crisis, and the number of people that went bankrupt due to not having enough savings to get by was staggering. You also want to save for the future. After all, at some point you will retire, and it'll be important to have a nest egg put away that you can tap into. Finally, you may want to go on vacation, purchase a new television, or even help pay for your children's college education. For all these reasons, it's very important to learn how to save. Think about it this way: If you cannot afford to purchase a television with cash, then going forward you won't be able to purchase a television until you have saved up for it.

Now, I also know many debt gurus tell you to pay off all your debt *before* you start saving. I personally disagree with this for a few reasons. First, if it takes you five years to pay off your debt and you don't save anything, you will likely take longer to pay off that debt than five years because life will get in the way, as it inevitably tends to do. Further, if you haven't saved for five years, then that's five years of compounded increase you have lost out on because you didn't have money in a fund or a product that grows the savings for the future. So, finding a way to save money is going to be extremely important.

Just like we did before, it is really important to look at your incoming versus your outgoing money and determine how much you want to save and for what you want to save. It's also important to divide up your savings into different buckets, all of which I will address. Finally, it's important to remember that the initial pain you will feel will be far surpassed by the joy of having something put away for the future, or for a key purchase.

# 20

# Going Cashless

While what I'm going to suggest is not truly going cashless, the sentiment is going to be the same. Before the advent of credit cards, there was a time when making a large purchase was accomplished by putting the item on *layaway*. In essence, you were using credit the store was giving you to have them hold the item in their inventory while you made payments towards purchasing it. The difference being that you did not receive the item until it was completely paid for. While in some ways this was a potential hardship for the retailer, but for you as a consumer it was great because you paid what you could afford to over a period of time. You were basically saving up for the item you wanted to purchase by giving the savings over directly to the store with the item you wanted. It's brilliant because you had to keep your eyes on the prize, and you weren't tempted to spend the savings on anything else because you were turning them over to the store. For the consumer, the biggest mistake a retailer made was to let you go home with a purchase you hadn't paid for, which eventually became "credit" and led to credit cards. If you had to pay for the purchase fully before you got to take it home, it disciplined you much more and you kept a firmer handle on your wallet. As it turns out, our grandparents' generation actually had it right!

I actually miss the concept of the layaway, and to be fair I use the principle to this day to help me save. If I can't afford what I want in one shot, I pay for it over a period of time, and I only get it when I have paid it off. The best example I can give you is when I purchase a family vacation. Because there are six of us, it can be quite expensive to go on a cruise. Simply reserving the space on the ship can be costly. Our principle has always been to look at the cost, divide it by twelve payments, and then provide the first payment to the cruise line. Every month they hit my charge card, which I pay off monthly, with an amount I can afford to pay. This forces me to live within my means and save up for a pretty fantastic trip every single year. It also means I show up on the trip with a fully paid-off vacation. Unlike many who book and pay for it on credit and live on credit throughout their trip, ours is paid off and we can truly enjoy the entire vacation. In this next section I'm going to give you a few tips and tricks on how to save money for major purchases and for long-term savings. As always, only you can take the first step to save, but if you do it, it will be worthwhile.

# 21

# Credit Cards and Charge Cards

I've already explained the differences between credit cards and charge cards. I want to be crystal clear how this is more than a personal preference—it's a way to really take control of your spending.

Remember, a credit card is a card that gives you a an amount of credit you can draw on and allows you to carry a balance from month to month in return for interest you will pay on any balance carried into the next month. And in some cases, especially down the road, it can be useful.

A charge card may or may not give you a limit, but it certainly does *not* allow you to carry a balance from month to month, and the interest they charge is quite punitive if by chance you miss your payment date. It's meant to give you the freedom to make the purchases you need while staying within your means because it must be paid off each month.

A charge card can be any from any company, including Visa, Mastercard, and American Express. So, if you have a favorite, you're able to choose the one you want. These cards can also provide you with points and perks just like a standard credit card does. The biggest and key item you need to be really clear on is that the charge card must be paid at the end of the month, and you need to monitor like a hawk and truly understand what and how much you can spend in a month. In the beginning, I would suggest applying for a charge card that will only give you a certain limit that is adequate enough to you for your monthly spend. So, if you spend $4, 000 a month, then that needs to be your limit, not less. In reality, even with poor credit, this shouldn't be a big issue.

See the Call to Action below to find assistance with this.

As previously discussed, you also need to commit to moving your regular bill spending to your charge card so you can fully see it, understand it, and let it automatically limit how much you can spend. The goal here is to not fall behind on a monthly basis, and not to spend more than you have. So, if the majority of all your bills hit your charge card and you know you can only spend $4,000 a month, the effect will first be to limit what you can spend your "free" money on. I know it's somewhat counterintuitive, but this is a very important principle: By limiting the amount you actually can spend, you will be able to stay within your means. By contrast, a credit card that allows you to spend up a limit that you don't have to pay off at the end of the month is just playing with fire, and you already know all too well whether or not you have the discipline to not carry a balance. The fact you're still reading this book indicates you need help with this. If you can grab hold of this one distinct principle, you will be far ahead of the curve and most other people.

## CALL TO ACTION

Go to www.scorebydnd.com and you can learn and now apply for the the Score Card by DND. You can apply for the credit limit you need and apply all the tips and hacks we have discussed throughout this book.

# 22

# Planning for Your Future

Once you have a charge card and have put your credit cards away, also known as pulling them out of your wallet, you need to get clear on how many different buckets you want for your savings. Is it saving for the future? Is it saving for a TV? Whatever it is, you need to set up goals. You also need to know how much you need to spend on a monthly basis for all your normal expenses (groceries, fuel, dinners out, and so on). Also, be ready to give some stuff up. If you are going to buy a television that will be $200 a month of your usual spending you will need to cut—yes, $200 worth of regular spending. The good thing is I promise you if you do this right, you won't really notice the loss of the extras, and as long as you have a budget as to what your regular bills are, you should not have any issues on making your regular payments. What you may not be able to do, though, is to live the same lifestyle you did before. You may have to drop the number of nights you go out to eat, or go drinking, or you may need to limit how much you spend on Lego sets, but the point is that there will have to be some give, but it won't be on the most important items.

Go to the Call to Action at the end of this chapter to get your free download!

Here is how you make this principle work: You ensure that the special savings you are doing hit your charge card on the day your new statement starts. If your card's "flip date" is the 14th of the month, then on the 15th you need to have the card billed for any large purchase you are saving for, such as a holiday. In this way the funds are taken out first, then have your regular bills charged to your card. Once those have both occurred, then the remaining you have left is yours to spend as you see fit. Except that we have only discussed how to save money for a one-time large purchase. How do we save for the longer term?

I alluded to this earlier in the book: Your savings will need to come from your card at the start. The reason for this is because it will lower the amount of money you will be spending out in the marketplace. When I was saving for my mortgage, I used to have a friend of mine run my card and then deposit the money into a separate account to keep from spending it. It lowered the amount I could spend monthly and it forced savings into my hands, but out of easy reach. You have to find your own way to do that, and you have to take the meaning you have to determine how much you want to save and with whom. It's not for me to tell you *where* to put your savings as an investment, but I want to give you a few tips on *how* to save. Many funds today can and will take a set amount off your charge card, so you don't need to have a friend do it like I did years and years ago. Also, some cards will allow you to take a cash advance (for a fee, of course), and finally you could go the friend route if you had to. The most important thing you can do is to decide *how much* you want to save and that you want to start saving *now*. If you can do that, you will find a way to save. The biggest trick, though, isn't getting the money off of your card—it's banking it.

So, you're taking your savings off of your charge card because the funds taken will limit how much you can waste in a month. It's an important concept, but what do you do when you get the funds in your hands? For example, if you don't have a friend who can run your card and your chosen investment vehicle cannot run your card, what do you do? Well, you can at least get started by working the cash advance method, which will cost you interest, but it won't be a serious amount. You then need to deposit the money at a *different bank than your regular bank*, and ensure you don't have easy access to the account. It's from that account you can have your investment fund take the money for longer-term savings.

Working in this way, the funds taken from your card, however you get them, aren't being mingled into your personal accounts that you use on a day-by-day basis. This will allow you to have the peace of mind that money is being saved. However, it's likely you aren't saving a lot of money. Do not get discouraged! You will be able to increase this without it feeling difficult. How, you ask? Easily, because you are *spending* your way to savings! The hit or high you get from using your card remains with you. Because you have determined to live within your means, you aren't spending more than you can pay off monthly, and because a portion of your monthly income is going towards paying off your credit cards, you aren't spending more than you have in hand. So, what happens when you actually pay off your credit cards, because believe me it will eventually happen!

There are a few options available to you. I would suggest the following: All the money you have been using to pay off your credit cards should then be put into that other account from where your long-term savings are being taken. You aren't going to notice a change in lifestyle at all! After all, you haven't had access to these funds in a few years, so once your debt has been paid down, then the amount you have been spending can go against your savings. If you were putting just $2,000 against your credit card debt a month, then that means after they're paid off you'll be saving $24,000 a year! And if it's was $3,000 per month, then you are looking at $36,000 in savings! And if it was $5,000 (which is a massive amount, I admit), then you'd be looking at saving $60,000 a year.

In this way without changing the amount you are spending, you are able to save and to save a significant amount. This doesn't include any raises you might get, or increases in income due to your business doing better. I have simply shown you how to pay off your debt and to save without increasing your income. And your income will likely increase over time as well. When this happens, your disposable income has increased, but you have good habits in place and are still not over-spending.

In the case of income increases, my serious suggestion is that you take ten percent of your increase and you add that to your savings. This is new money to you, and if you create the habit to do this right away, you will never miss a measly ten percent of your income, and yet it will make a *massive* difference to you over the long haul, especially if you are younger. In fact, the younger you are the more your savings will affect your ability to have money in the future. But don't kid yourself, because while the best time to save was ten years ago (which is always the case), the second-best time is *now*! In fact, I suggest that every year you look at your expenses and determine how or where you can cut some costs. Do you really need three landline phones? And any such amounts you can find, after you have started your debt freedom plan, should go straight to savings.

## CALL TO ACTION

Go to www.scorebydnd.com/debttowealth and enter the code exercise8 to complete the form and download the free worksheet from our website.

# 23

# You Can Change the Conversation

You can have savings, you can buy a new home, or a new car, but it's not going to happen overnight. It will take time and work. In this case, time is definitely on your side. I want to ensure you understand, though, that *you can change the conversation*, you can do things that perhaps you thought you could not do before. I'm not suggesting it will be easy or won't take work, but you can absolutely pay off your debt, save for the future, and keep your credit rating in a good standing.

You have to believe this, because if you don't then you won't be willing to put the work in, but if you do believe it, you will be able to delay your gratification long enough to start and finish with your financial goals.

Don't beat yourself up, either. This is not an easy course of action, and you may find that sometimes you fail. The important thing is to get back on the horse and really and truly keep to the plan you have crafted. The beauty of this plan is that you don't spend more than you have, and the money you are already putting towards your debt will be used to fuel your debt payments and eventually your savings.

Even if you have very little or no savings, this isn't an unrealistic plan for you. I already described what household debt looks like in three countries. If you are in another country, chances are it's just as bad, especially in most western countries. So, it's up to you to be willing to change the conversation and fix your own household.

# 24

# How to Move to Cash
# Without the Cash

In previous chapters, I described the importance of a charge card and the need to move away from cash purchases. I want to further reflect on this with you now.

Why am I telling you to move everything you can to a charge card, and out of your bank account, and why am I telling you to avoid cash where possible? There are a number of reasons, but the key reasoning is this: If you set an upper limit on your card, this will prevent you from going over your spending capability. Furthermore, if you move all bills possible to your card, then you will have a much more detailed and easy-to-access accounting, especially at the end of the month, of where your money goes. Finally, by avoiding cash where possible, or journaling every time you spend, you will avoid leakage. What I mean by leakage is when money disappears and you don't really know why or where it goes.

When I was young, I was pretty insane in my wife's eyes because when we went on holiday I would take a specific amount of money and I would write out EVERY SINGLE cent spent. Twenty-five cents on a post card? I wrote it down. Five bucks on snacks? I wrote it down. Whatever it was that came out of cash, I wrote it down and then I tallied it at the end of the day. I actually had an envelope on the front of which I wrote out the spending by day, and inside I put the receipts in order. This allowed me to have full control of what was being spent, and to plan for the future. If I knew I spent $100 a day on touring and I only brought $500 for a week-long trip, then I would know I was in trouble. It also forced me to think about every single purchase. You'll find I don't spend money on frivolous items. I just don't do it. You may think I was crazy, but I will promise you this, I knew where every dollar went!

Conversely, nowadays if I don't write out everything that is being spent, I have no idea where the money goes, especially if I have cash in hand. While cash is great because you only spend what you have in hand, if you don't have good spending habits then you will waste it or lose it. A fool and his money are soon parted, after all. So, I strongly suggest that where at all possible, at least for the time being, you should avoid carrying cash. In today's world it's becoming less and less necessary to carry cash. But a word of caution: I am not suggesting you spend like crazy on your cards because you don't have cash! I am suggesting you use that dreaded curse word, you know, *discipline*, to gauge your spending. It's to this end that I am also suggesting you don't pull out your debit card. You need to be consistent on how you are spending. Over time you will gain the discipline you need to use debit and cash, but for now I suggest avoiding it. The problem, of course, is that as humans we suck at discipline, so I am offering you something even better than discipline—I'm offering a way to set up regular routines so that when this all becomes habit, you won't even have to think about what you are doing. It will become subconscious, and it's at that point you won't even need to be disciplined because you will just be going through your daily and weekly routine, your normal habits of life. And that's what will keep it all sustainable.

# 25

# Living Within Your Means

One of the most important parts of this discussion is you learning to live within your means. This isn't as difficult, or as easy, as it sounds or seems. If you have been notoriously living above your means for a long time, it will be extremely difficult to change your habits, but it will also be extremely rewarding to do so. If you haven't realized it by now, the main driver to change is your *mental attitude*. If you *believe* you can live within your means—cut back a little on expenses, pursue debt freedom, savings, and keeping your credit in good shape— then you absolutely can do it. If you *don't* believe you can do this, then you will fail.

Darren Hardy, in his book *The Compound Effect*, speaks to the fact that many people give up before results are even seen.[6] Think of it this way: If you want to run a 10K, you often don't start out being able to run 10K. In fact, many times you can't even run 1K! If that's the case, then you need to make decisions daily and weekly to ensure you get to the desired goal and trust that the compounding effect of training every day will pay off. It's the same way when you look at your retirement account. You may desire to to stop putting money into retirement savings after only a few years because $5,000 a year may not feel like it's adding up to much savings, but when

---

6   See https://darrenhardy.com/the-compound-effect-resources

you realize the effect of interest compounding on your savings, you will see at retirement that suddenly you have a nice nest egg, even though in the day-to-day it doesn't seem that way. It's the same when you decide to live within your means. It doesn't seem like much when you make that decision to not go out to dinner or order take out, but if you stick with it, keep to it, and work your plan, then you will find over time that you have more savings, more debt being paid off, and more to work with moving forward. You just have to be patient enough to see those results.

Living and spending within your means is going to make a difference, and it will have a massive impact on your life. Sadly, you likely won't notice it for a while, or you'll only notice the negative side of the equation, such as "Oh, I can't order that pizza, I have to cook one instead" or "I'm sorry, I can't go out to dinner because I'm saving to pay off my credit card." None of these are easy things to say or do, but as you do it and repeat it, you will come to realize what is important to you. Maybe you do need to have a dinner out once a month. As a tradeoff though, maybe you'll be happy to give up your Netflix subscription.

As I write this, I get more excited about how I can *keep* more instead of *spend* more. To that end, I just cancelled my Amazon Prime membership! About six months ago I ordered a product and inadvertently signed myself up for Amazon Prime. Every month I was being charged for Prime membership. I realized I needed to drop it. It wasn't easy because we got used to watching great programs and movies on Prime Video and using Prime for faster ordering and free shipping. But then I realized I already have Netflix and Spotify, which made Prime just a waste of money. Granted, the Prime membership was "only" $7.99 a month, but that's $95.88 a year. You may think, why bother making such a small decision? I'll give you two reasons: First, we honestly did not need Prime. We didn't use it enough to justify having it. I was keeping it as an insurance, in case there was nothing on Netflix to watch (by the way I cancelled basic cable ages ago). Second, I decided to cancel it because by doing so I can justify cancelling anything I am not using and I can stop the leakage, meaning the leakage of my finances from my pocket to someone else's! An extra benefit is that the $95.88 could now enter the budget and be used for savings, for a dinner with the kids, or an order-in night. It was free money. In other words, why *not* make that small decision?

Here's an important point I want to make: These seemingly small decisions to make simple changes often never happen for most people. Why? They are stuck in a state of inertia. They resist change. Even these kinds of small decisions require you to consciously overcome the inertia and natural resistance to change. In the case of cancelling Prime, I had to go and DIG through the website to figure out how to cancel it. I then needed to click through no fewer than four different web pages confirming I no longer wanted Prime. And then I got an email touting all the reasons I should come back!

My point is this: When you want to make a change, say to cancel your cable, for example, it won't be made easy for you. When we did it, we had to call the cable company to get permission to cancel, listen to all the ways they tried to rescue us from what would clearly be a life devoid of all meaning without cable, and then return all the equipment to them AND accept a higher cost for our internet because we no longer had a bundle. It was maddening! However, by cancelling I saved somewhere in the region of $150 a month plus tax, even after my internet bill increased. That meant $1,800 a year plus the taxes I paid on it. My internet went up by $20 a month. So, I had a net savings of $130 a month, which for the year became $1,680 saved. With taxes in Canada it ended up being a grand total of $1,898.40 a year. I now had the chance to save this money, save part of it, or even spend it on dinners out with my family. While neither you nor I will get rich over $130 a month, I will say the habit of saving that money for something else such as a better birthday gift for one of my kids, or simply putting it into long-term savings for the family, will make a massive difference over time. Why? Because you are actively choosing where you are putting your money, and you are compounding what it can do for you if you save it. Furthermore, the new thing you do with that money won't cause any pain because you were already spending that money! Whether you move it to savings, retire more debt, or anything else, you won't feel where that money went, *at all*. It was already being spent, so now it's just being spent elsewhere on something more productive.

If what you cut is something like cable, you may feel it at first because you are giving something up, and only you can determine how important that something is to you. I can honestly tell you that we didn't miss having cable at all. But we did sign up for Netflix at approximately $10 a month. That was more than enough for us, and in my case avoided wasting time on "bad TV" and resulted in less TV bleeding occurring in our lives. What I mean by that is this: We stopped watching news, we stopped watching TV shows we knew were no good for us, and stopped letting one bad show roll over into another because we were too lazy to shut the "boob tube" off, not to mention the incessant stream of commercials that come with cable television, all designed to get inside your head and convince you to buy things you really don't even need. I'm not anti-television, which would be hypocritical of me since we have Netflix, but for me and my family cable television was simply something we didn't need to spend money on.

To recap, it's not easy to change, and when you do try to change there will be plenty of resistance. It's up to you to make those cuts and to make them work for you. If you run a company and you know there is waste in the business, the best thing you can do is cancel that payment or cost, even if it's a person! Being lean is a good thing.

# 26

# Budgeting

A topic I am sure everyone has been dreading but knew had to come up in detail in this book is *budgeting*. I can't even begin to describe how integral this will be to paying off your debt! It's a simple fact that if you have no idea how much you have coming in, and you have no clue what's going out, then you have no general idea of how you are spending your money. And there are too many people and companies out there that want to part you from your money. Netflix, Spotify, Amazon Prime, and on goes the list. None of these are evil or bad, but if you have all of them, then maybe that's exactly what they are for you.

Go to the Call to Action at the end of this chapter so you can download those resources!

I'll explain how I set up a budget, and whether this works for you or not only you can determine. First, I write out where every dollar goes, and this includes what I consider "free spending" or the leakage that inevitably happens when you have cash in hand. This is why I recommend going cash-free, because all those little purchases add up to significant sums over time. This is the hardest part of the budget, but you have to find out where your money goes. The second thing I add are the regular payments I know I am spending money on. I also write out mortgage/rent, any automatic savings—everything that comes out of my accounts. I then look at what is coming in on a separate piece of paper. And then I need to make some decisions.

First, it's just not wise to have every dollar that comes in also go out. It will never allow you to have a few dollars here and there, and while the idea *is* to save money, it's *not* to make yourself broke. Now that we are looking at ins and outs, we need to write out the outgoing payments in order of importance and try to look at them as percentages against your income. For example, I would not recommend having fifty percent of your income going to your mortgage or rent, which would indicate you're not in affordable housing.

Before I delve into this and give you a few pointers, I want to be really clear that my assumption is, entrepreneur or not, your tax is taken off your income at the source, meaning where you work, so when your paycheck comes into your account it is "free" to be spent.

I am also going to give you my own personal spin on things, just so you understand where I am coming from. I personally and fervently believe that a full ten percent of your income should go to charity. And yes, I also believe that ten percent should be calculated on your gross income before taxes are taken out. But this is me, because I believe we need to give back and to do it first before anything else happens. By taking it off the top, you won't notice it going out.

What's next? Let's take a closer look at your housing expense. If we look at mortgages, most banks will only allow you to spend 28% of your total monthly income towards your mortgage, and they also don't want to see more than 36% of your total monthly income going to total monthly debt. For a good source of information on this, visit the following link:

https://home.howstuffworks.com/real-estate/buying-home/what-is-debt-to-income-ratio-for-a-mortgage.htm

This is very much based on a North American perspective. If you are renting, there is a bit more flexibility—and ability to get yourself in trouble. Most experts would suggest you spend no more than 30% of your monthly income towards your rent. The problem here is two-fold: Most Americans spend closer to 50% of their income on housing, and as rental rates and property values continue to increase, this becomes more and more burdensome. A good source of information on can be found by visiting the following link:

https://budgeting.thenest.com/percentage-income-should-rent-31823.html

Here is the reality, though: If you are spending more than 30% in either case, whether rental or mortgage, you are "house-burdened" and will likely struggle to meet your financial obligations. I don't want to give you a full in-depth accounting class on why 30% is the magic number, nor what is included in it beyond stating that if you have a mortgage the banks will include your real estate taxes and insurance in this number. If you are renting then it's just your rental payment. If you can get this number down to 25% of your monthly income, then you will be considered to be living conservatively, and that's going to be a good thing.

When we look at the next set of spending, about 20% should be going towards fixed costs that simply don't change (or at least not much) over time, including car payments, utilities, and so on. These are the things you absolutely need for our survival and don't fluctuate much on a month-to-month basis.

The next 30% of your income is what is called "disposable income," and should go towards things that are more variable, such as groceries, clothing, entertainment, and so on. This is the area you will likely shrink the most, and the area you will need to keep a close eye on as well. While you need to buy groceries, you don't always need to buy potato chips. You don't have to go to the movies every week. You don't always need to buy new clothing, but you do want to ensure the ability to buy clothing is there when needed.

Finally, the last 20% goes towards savings and/or paying off debt. I won't spend too much time here now except to say this: At first glance, this is where most people don't put their money (savings and debt payoffs) and instead it goes either into housing or into the disposable income category of 30% described above. What you will need to do is to set up any savings to come out of your accounts right when you get paid, as discussed previously, and to ensure you can't access those funds easily. Further, hopefully, all the payments you are making towards debt repayment will fit into this number. The main thing here is to understand that if you work the plan I have discussed in this book and if you are already spending 20% of your income on debt/savings, you can and you will make it. The concern is if your number is either much higher or much lower, then you will need to work on it.

If the number is 30% of your income, it means you will need to be extremely aggressive at paying down your debt, which means you will have to give up some things until you get this number down to 20%. If the number is too low, you are likely not saving anything, and while you may be just making your monthly payments on the debt side, you may have to give up some nice-to-haves to bring this number up. The good news is you will pay your debt off faster, and you will save more money quicker.

The important thing here is that these are the suggestions made by financial gurus. It may not reflect where you are at right now, but finding out where you are at relative to these goalposts is paramount. Only then can you start making a plan for how get there.

I want to deal with a little bit of the nitty-gritty if I can, just from a habit-forming perspective, so you know how your spending can have the most bang for your buck.

I strongly suggest that any charitable giving you do happen *first*, because once it's spent, it's gone and you won't notice it, and it'll build a good, healthy habit of giving. If you try to do it last you will find there is "more month than money," and then it will be the thing you give up on first.

The next area to focus on is savings/debt. Follow the plan as discussed in this book and then whatever you are saving needs to go to those designated areas. By doing this you won't miss out on saving, and you will ensure the most important part of servicing and reducing your debt levels will occur.

Next, your housing and essential spending needs to be handled (car payment, insurance, utilities, and so on). These essential payments should be automatic, and hopefully are done using your charge card as previously discussed.

This will then leave you with hopefully 30% of your monthly income, but it could be less. This is going to be where you actually and truly need to *budget* because the items above really are not going to change much on a monthly basis. But this area can vary quite a bit. You will first need to decide what, if anything, you are getting rid of. Next, you need to sit down and work out what you are spending on things that are *important* but aren't in your *essential* spending group. How much do you spend on fuel and groceries, which are the absolute most important items in this area. Then you need to look at what's left and allocate it monthly—items like cable, internet, Netflix, and so on—how much are those costing you per month? Then how much are you spending outside the home? These are things like dinners, movies, clothing, entertainment, and so on. set a specific number that you will max out for the month.

You don't want to buy that extra drink at dinner and find out it prevented you from getting to work on the day before you get paid!

This will take constant work to monitor. I seriously suggest you always do your best to be reasonable here. While I have been talking about the need for discipline and to ensure you can pay off your debt, it's no good putting yourself in shackles and building a plan that makes you completely miserable all the time. We're still human and we need to have a bit of enjoyment in our lives! But I do caution you, if your cards are maxed out, you have already had that enjoyment, so now it needs to be not just within your means but minimal spending for the time being.

When you get good at budgeting in this area, what you should discover is that you have money left over at the end of the month! It may be $10 or it may be $100—it doesn't matter how much it is, but whatever is left over you need to withdraw and put into a separate account. Your idea may be to spend this, but don't! Instead, this can go to a rainy-day fund, or a savings fund for small purchases. After all, if you are saving *only* for long-term purposes as explained earlier, you won't be able to buy anything that is more than you can afford inside your monthly allowances. With this added twist of setting aside any leftover money, you can save it for smaller significant purchases, such as a $300 bicycle, which you could save up in a matter of months using this approach. The key is putting that money in a separate account to prevent you from spending it. It will force you to delay your gratification, but in doing so you will have the joy of knowing you paid cash for the item.

If you have an exceptionally good month, I suggest you put a good portion of it against the lowest-balance credit card in order to pay it off faster, or put it into a longer-term savings account so the temptation to spend it doesn't occur.

A quick note about hitting goals because I feel it is worthwhile to speak to it here. As you pay off your credit cards and depending on how many you have, it may just get really depressing and demotivating to not be able to spend a little or to celebrate a win. I seriously suggest you set out small rewards you can execute on that will give you and your partner/family great joy. For example, if you are like us and you are a rock climber and you feel your climbing shoes are getting old and worn out, you may then set this as goal: When I pay off this $2,500 credit card I'm going to spend $100 on new climbing shoes. This sets a clear, definite, realistic, and not out-of-whack goal to your debt/savings plan. But you need to be careful that the celebration doesn't negate what you just did in paying off your debt! You don't want to be like my friend who rewarded himself for not smoking for twelve months by having a cigarette! Years later he is still smoking, and that's because he went backwards. So, this goal needs to be clearly thought-out, and must be something you save for on the side, like that bicycle I mentioned above. It must not be on your card; it must be out of free "saved" monies. You will find this works, and it will be a good motivation to get the next debt paid off.

## CALL TO ACTION

Go to www.scorebydnd.com/debttowealth and enter the code exercise9 to complete the form and download the free worksheets from our website.

I've discussed the *why* of paying down your debt and the *how* of paying down your debt and saving. I want to now start transitioning to some higher thought processes you'll find are very useful on your journey.

# 27

# The Buckets: Visualizing Where to Put What

I like the word *buckets* because from a visual perspective it conveys the right idea. There are a bunch of different areas where you will place your funds. In recent conversations I've had this discussion with up-and-coming successful people about the importance of why having *more* accounts is always better than having *fewer* accounts. Having fewer accounts leads to the potential of not saving what you need to save and not putting aside what you need to put aside. The more accounts, the better off you are. Having accounts at several different banks is ideal. However, a strong caveat here is to get the free, cheapie no-fee accounts. Don't end up burdening yourself with accounts that charge you an arm and a leg to have them.

Here is the world according to Garp (a very obscure reference I suggest you check out): When all your funds are in one bank account and you aren't always paying attention to what is going in and what is going out, then the general feeling is well, when it's gone, it's gone. And anything left over is almost always going to be spent because it was just sitting there. Here is the proof, and I asked this of you earlier, what do you save at the end of the month? Anything? If not, you likely are using only one bank account.

Here is what I do: I have my main account, which is for "everyday" items, where paychecks from my company are deposited and where I have a checkbook. My next account is where my "immediate" savings are drawn from. The idea here is that when my paycheck comes in, I transfer the required funds into that account immediately. I also have a separate account for my mortgage, and again the transfer is done on the first day I receive my paycheck. I pay my charge card next (assuming you have set it up to have a due date in this time period) because I use it for my charitable donations and all my regular expenses so I can monitor what is going through it. I next have accounts for my kids and my wife. My kids' accounts take their savings almost immediately, and my wife's account is so she has funds for whatever she may require (and this is pre-planned, pre-budgeted, and agreed upon and isn't for items that would go on the charge card she holds), and in turn she has a separate account at another bank that she transfers funds to that I have no oversight on so she can plan and do whatever she wants to with her money. Thereafter, I have a second bank where I have a personal account, a joint account, accounts for each of my kids, and an alternate savings account. Here is how they work:

For my kids I put away a certain amount every month, the immediate savings goes in the first bank, however I have a second amount, including birthday money and so forth, that goes into a second bank which once a year I put into an investment for them, which in my case is a twenty-year pay insurance, which simply means it's an insurance that's paid off in twenty years, is over-paid to ensure there is savings in there, and the hope is it will help with college when the time comes. My alternate savings account is for when I want to make a purchase and I take the money from bank 1 and put it into bank 2 so I don't notice it and I've effectively "spent" the money early, so it simply accumulates there. The main account is where everything is deposited into and dispersed through and the joint account is where I put in any cash monthly savings for a rainy day that I have been able to slowly develop. This amount can be small or large, but we have a goal as to how much we want to save into this account, something we as a couple feel comfortable with, and monthly we deposit funds into this account. This is also the account that at the end of the month, if there is anything in our personal account at bank 1 when our next paycheck comes in, we transfer it into this account. We do It by check because effectively I'm "spending" the money and getting a dopamine hit from spending, but I'm spending it into my own accounts, and the "high" I'm getting is from *saving*. But my brain simply sees it as *spending*.

You will have lots and lots of bank accounts, and some will have funds in them and some will not. By doing this, though, the account that is connected to your debit card, or acts rather as your main card, will act as a limiter to you and you won't have much in that account except for truly disposable income, that percentage we discussed a few chapters ago, that you can spend.

A further proviso: If you can't move all your payments to your charge card, then open another bank account for those payments, with the amounts to pay them transferred over when you get paid like you do your mortgage.

Why do this? First, it's going to show you how little you really have as disposable income, which is the same for all of us. Second, it's going to ensure all your main bills are paid in a timely and orderly fashion. Finally, it will also starkly show you if you are living above your means. If after doing your regular monthly spending (all your savings, paying your charge card, putting aside the funds for mortgage and payments that can't go on your charge card) you have no money left, then you are living above your means and you need to tweak your plan.

This new method of having many accounts may seem tedious and a lot of work when you first start, but it will pay big dividends over time, especially if you are able to start getting to a point where you can start putting money away every month without noticing it. That money is always better in your bank account than it is in the hands of the restaurant, the clothing boutique, or the cable man, because not one of those will ever pay your bills or ensure you have savings for the future!

## CALL TO ACTION

Go to www.scorebydnd.com/debttowealth and enter the code exercise10 to complete the form and download the free worksheet from our website.

# 28

# Charitable Giving

I have covered how to get out of debt and save money, and how to keep your credit rating higher. I have only mentioned giving money away to charity in passing, so I want to expand on that for a bit here.

I know many people are going to say something like, "Hang on there, Bill, I can't afford to pay off my credit cards and save money *and* give money away!" Yes, I seriously want you to think about it, and yes you *can* do it. When you give to something, anything greater than yourself, it's like telling the world, the whole universe even, that you know no matter how great or bad things are for you, there is something or someone out there that needs help, and you're willing to step up. You become part of a greater culture and community of *compassion*. The habit it instils in your spending is pretty amazing as well, because the first thing you learn is if you can't live on 90% of your income, you can't live on 100% of it. However, if you can learn to live on 90% of it, then you can learn to actually work with the number and to push it down as required. As it turns out, giving is also good for your health. Finding a cause you believe in that you want and need to give to, gives you a feeling of joy and happiness (and who doesn't need a little more of that?), and you feel better about yourself. This is because you have joined that larger community and you are involved in seeing it through. This is a pretty important thing because if you get to a point where you are feeling down you can always remind yourself of those you are helping.

Regarding who or what you should give to, that's up to you. As for me, I'm a God-fearing and God-loving kind of guy, so I have some very particular opinions on this, and to that end my wife and I make most of our charitable giving to the church. But you aren't me, and you don't have to give as I give. Thus, I don't much care if your giving is to save the whales, or to feed starving children in Africa, though I do have opinions about such things. But the important thing is that you are giving and reaching out to those that need your help and you are assisting them. Hopefully, you'll gain some fire out of it and will want to help physically as well. However, from a financial perspective the idea is that by giving you are putting a stake in the ground to say I can live off of less and I will, in order to help others. As I was saying earlier, your giving needs to come *first* in your payments monthly. And I personally believe 10% is the number you need to look at giving. Many people I know far exceed that, but I think it's a good place to start.

As you move on to getting out of debt, putting savings in the bank, and repairing your credit, or keeping it where it is, you'll learn that this isn't an overnight journey. This is probably going to take at least a few years, so wouldn't you like to be a better person as you complete this journey? By giving you have the opportunity to do that.

# 29

# Summary

Before we move on to the last section of this book I wanted to take a breath to review where we've been so far and some of the key points covered.

You likely have multiple credit cards, and while this isn't terrible, what you want to do is move to a charge card or two as you pay off those credit cards. When you have completely paid them down, then having only one credit card that you use in case you need to carry a balance for a specific item will be fine, because by then you will have the habit in place to pay down on a specific basis. Any other cards should be charge cards.

All of your payments as much as possible should go through your charge card, with only items such as rent/mortgage, savings, or others you simply cannot move to your charge card going through your accounts.

Setting up separate accounts is critical, including a main account, and others for your rent/mortgage, your savings, your essential non-card payments, and then a separate bank with accounts for various kinds of savings accounts, all of which will assist you in saving money. And don't forget to transfer whatever is left over in your main account at the end of the month into your savings accounts! For extra credit, set up a cash savings account for a rainy day fund or medium-term purchases you want to make in cash, and keep it in the second bank.

When you are looking to pay off your credit, use the technique of paying minimums on everything, pulling off the amounts you have paid as a cash advance and placing it all on the lowest-balance card until it's paid off, then rinse and repeat. Do not cancel your credit cards until all your debt is paid off, and then you can look at what you truly do and don't need from a credit perspective, and reduce your credit only from a position of strength.

Don't forget to set goals and celebrate wins along the way—small goals and rewards, not trips to Italy! However, the human spirit requires constant feedback and positive reinforcement. To that end, every time you pay down a card give yourself a reward that you for pay in money you have saved up, in essence "cash," and keep it commensurate.

When you have paid off your cards, keep taking that money aside and start adding it to your savings, you won't miss the money as you've already been spending it all this time.

And the most important point of all because it's the most impactful, remember you can't go anywhere unless you *know your starting point*. Thus, write down your net-worth statement, your debt statement, your financial goals, and your spending requirements monthly. Make some hard choices as to what you can or cannot remove from your spending to assist you in paying down your debt.

## CALL TO ACTION

Bill is available to come to your area to speak on this important topic if you or a group you know could benefit from this. Email us at speaking@scorecardbydnd.com to book him today! And don't forget to download all the resources while you are there!

# Part III

## Advanced Techniques: Credit for Your Small Business

# 30

# You Aren't that Different

Initially, I think it's very important to realize that small business credit grantors don't really view you as a person any different from your business. In some ways, your business is very much an extension of yourself. If you are a sole proprietor this is simply the fact of the matter, and everything I previously covered above applies directly to you and your business. If we look at a partnership, you actually get to contend with your partner's bad decisions along with your own. However, if we focus on an incorporated business, there are a number of differences to be aware of and to understand how you are seen, especially when initially your business is seen as an extension of yourself.

It's important to first understand that when you incorporate your business, legally it is seen as a separate entity with its own credit profile and its own history. A company would then rely on its financial statement to ensure it's a stable entity, except that in the early days your business will not have a financial statement or credit history, but it will have *you*. So, you will have to provide any credit grantor your *personal* details in order to receive even the smallest loan or line of credit for your business. Whether it's $1,000 to an office supply company or it's $25,000 for computer equipment, it will be *your* name and *your* history that will have to provide the backup and the strength for the company.

I don't want to belabor the differences between the various kinds of companies, but I will provide a little information here and now. As a self-employed sole proprietor, basically everything described earlier in this book applies to the business, and any lender will simply look at all your personal finances to decide. This is because there is no difference between your business and yourself, you are the same person. As a partnership, it is you personally and your partner personally whose histories together will either strengthen or weaken your ability to obtain credit. From a credit granting process there is very little to add. While there are many reasons to choose a specific kind of business entity, those details are beyond the scope of this book, so the assumption here is you have already made this choice.

As a company, when you start the business, regardless of the number of owners, it will be the personal strength of the individuals that will become the focus at a number of different times when looking at the credit process and this is what I want to cover.

First, when you start your company and are seeking credit, your company will require your own and your fellow founders' credit strength to stand behind the company. Therefore, as described when you are in a personal good situation, you want to have a solid credit report because this will allow your company to have a solid credit report based on you and your founders. A few points to note: In more than twenty years I've never seen a company have good credit while its founder has bad credit when they are tied together personally. This could happen much further along when the company is no longer reliant on the owner, but that is a different circumstance. As the owner pays their own credit, that is generally seen as how they will also fulfil their corporate responsibilities. Further, it only takes one bad apple to ruin the whole bunch, one poor credit situation in a group of three owners will or could ruin it for the group. Be aware with whom you are doing business!

To be clear, when I state you need to stand behind your company, it means you are offering your personal guarantee. This means if the company fails to pay its obligations, *you* are agreeing to take responsibility for making good on the payment. Hence, if you already don't pay your bills well, are maxed out, or have a bad credit rating, you will have a more difficult time having your company get the credit it may need.

A company can only gain credit, at least at the start, based on you and your other owners' strength. This can change after about three years of operations and then profitability in the company. If the company is profitable, then you may not need to continue to offer your personal guarantee unless, of course, you are looking for a substantial amount of credit or your profits are not strong enough to support the lending you need. If that is the case, you will again be asked for your personal guarantee. This is pretty normal for an entrepreneur to be in this position until the business becomes successful enough to stand on its own two feet. Please just be aware that if the debt is large enough, you can open yourself up to being sued and held responsible for the entire debt personally.

# 31

# Get Yourself Right and Your Company will Follow

If you truly ensure you get yourself right by paying off debt, saving money, managing your credit rating, then your company will follow suit. This is because you will start to do the same thing with your company, using the same personal habits you've developed with your company. It's these habits taken into your company that will pay you dividends in the future. The most important thing I can tell you is that it won't happen overnight. It will take time and effort to make it happen, especially if you have a long way to come from personally.

However, use the same thoughts and processes covered throughout this book. Look at the financial and net-worth statements of your company, look at the incoming and the outgoing money, and look at what you can realistically cut out. You need to get to a point where you are living within your means. Now a proviso: I don't know your business. Maybe you are some tech company with a plan and a burn rate and you know what you are doing in these areas. If so, feel free to ignore what I am talking about. This is more for those who don't have any white knights or fat wallets propping them up and need to make some cold hard decisions.

By ensuring your company is living within its means, you are first ensuring you are not living on debt. From there you need to ensure that out of whatever funds come in you immediately set aside all statutory payments you'll need to make, including taxes, employee deductions, sales tax, and so on. After all, the money for these isn't your money, it's the government's money, and the government is one creditor you know will pierce any corporate veil and come after you personally. Don't mess with them.

After that, you may realize you are spending more than you can afford. There are many much better accounting books and authors who will walk you through having a profitable business, so I'm not even going to attempt to do that here for you. What I am going to say is that this isn't going to work for you in the longer term unless you are fabulous at fundraising! So, you will need to determine what needs to be cut and maybe it will take you some time to do so. I'm just encouraging you to get off your credit cards and your debt instruments and use them for what they were meant for, which is short-term financing. I'm a big believer in making small incremental changes that will lead to long-term bigger changes as opposed to trying to change everything all at once. Ripping the band aid off, while mentally a good practice, may not work in your company. If you have a staff of five and can only afford two, it probably wouldn't be wise to fire three people on the same day if you haven't figured out how their job duties will be covered moving forward. You also may not be able to back out of some contracts with vendors right away. These details are beyond the scope of this book and I encourage you to talk to the right people. There is always an option and a way to make it work; you just have to look to find the way forward.

# 32

# Trade Creditors

Your trade creditors or vendors are very much like your personal credit cards. They will report your payment history to the credit agencies and you need to be aware of this. Before credit facilities were very popular, it was your reputation with your vendors that determined whether people would do business with you or not. Thus, ensuring your vendors are paid, and paid within terms, will ensure your corporate reputation is kept in good standing.

A great vendor reference will often allow you to open up new accounts with other merchants, especially in the absence of either a solid bank account or financial statement. So, if you pay your vendors on time and within the terms of your agreement, this will have a very positive impact on your "corporate credit." Maintaining a good relationship with these creditors will also often give you a leg up over your competitors, who may not always treat them as well. Furthermore, when you need assistance, or a larger extension of credit, your positive past payment history will hopefully allow them to extend more favorable terms to you.

A note, however: Don't be afraid to shop around when it comes to vendors. When I first started in business, I had a set of accountants and I am not ashamed to say I was slow in payments, but they too were slow in performing their duties for us. In part this was because the partner we had was undergoing family difficulties. We were moved to a new partner who, in his words, "brought and kept our account up to date" and kept it that way by insisting we pay 50% of our fees upfront. At the time we had seven companies and paid in excess of $70,000 a year to these accountants, plus my personal fees as well. there were a few years where I started to question these costs, but was told this was how it had to be. When we went through a difficult year, as inevitably happens in the finance business, we wanted to pay after the accounts were completed but this partner refused to make any sort of arrangements with us! This was in spite of our company having been a stellar and large client of this firm for many years, and our previous "problem status" had been removed for well over ten years. This prompted me to look to other firms, and I quickly discovered that we were way overpaying for their services. In fact, in the first year of our move to a new accounting firm, we saved 50% of the fees we were paying to the former firm. This caused this partner to reach out to family to convince them we had made a mistake in moving our business because our entire family used this firm and I am a partner in one of my companies with my brother. I refused to return on the basis of what I was being charged by them and their unwillingness to work with us.

What's the moral of the story? 1) Build up a great reputation with your vendors. 2) If they won't work with you, then don't feel bad about moving on. 3) Shop around and keep them honest.

P.S. I didn't return to them, despite much family pressure to do so. Eventually, other members of my family moved key accounts from them as well, because when things are great, certain costs aren't noticed, but when you have to look at the bottom line and everything is suspect, being over-charged by a vendor, especially accountants who are paid to help you, that becomes inexcusable.

# 33

# Living Within Your Means Revisited

This leads to my biggest item for the corporate section, and the most important one, just as it is in the personal one is this: You have to live within your means. This means taking a hard look at your incoming versus your outgoing money and making some hard choices. In your company it may be possible due to the way you are funded, and perhaps based on your model, to let higher costs that outstrip your profits to ride, but in most cases this simply leads to you closing your doors.

In most cases you cannot afford to spend more than you earn, especially because then you cannot pay yourself! It also means you cannot spend all the way UP to how much you bring in, because you need to make payroll, taxes, and save so there is equity in your company and then some. Trying to explain how you should save is not my area of expertise, or how much of income should go towards operational expenses, payroll, and so on. I will only go so far as to say that in most cases you cannot survive if you are spending more than you are making. It's just not possible, and in this case spending more than you are making needs to include your bills, your payroll, and your taxes, and it must also include anything you are putting aside in your company to hold as equity, you need to build something into your business you are *not* spending.

Whether you call it a float or whether you are calling it equity in the business, you need to keep something in the business. The positive funds you keep in the business attest to your tangible net worth and will help you build your long-term profitable growth. It will also help other companies see there is value in your business and eventually it's worth lending to it.

# 34

# Multiple Bank Accounts

Just like in your personal life, your corporate life needs more than one bank account. Mike Michalowicz's book *Profit First* details this really well and I don't even want to attempt to rehash what he has written, except to say I agree with him.[7] The more bank accounts with purpose the better.

When I first started in business I did not put money aside for my quarterly tax remittance and when it was due at the end of the quarter I had to scramble to get it paid. After dealing with that twice, I opened up a new account and every payment that came in I took the tax amount and started paying it into a second account. No longer would I have to worry about tax as I wasn't going to spend it. I continued this when it was time to put aside funds for corporate payroll remittances, the staff portion, and other things as well—every key payment got an account. Some accounts were created in different banks so I didn't even know they existed in order to prevent spending and of it. I lived what Mike's book discusses and I can tell you it works, and I wholeheartedly endorse his concept of having multiple bank accounts. I simply stumbled upon it myself on my own, years before he wrote the book. I also want to recommend the book I because it is spot-on with all its advice.

---

[7]  See https://mikemichalowicz.com/profit-first.

The more accounts you can have for all the key areas of your business, just like in your personal life, the more likely you will be able to set yourself up for success.

# 35

# Don't Overextend Your Expenses

It's tempting as you are growing your business, especially as a small business, to not pay attention to the monthly expenses and to live via your cash flows. In other words, if you have the funds in the cash register or the bank accounts, then you can afford to make the next purchase. I really want to encourage you to look deeper than this; to look towards a cash flow statement, and there are many simple computer programs and bookkeepers to help you do this. You need to really and truly understand what is your profit, what is your working capital, and what needs to be held in reserves before you are simply spending on your next invoice. You may find you have less money than you think you have to spend, or you may have more money than you think you have to spend (wouldn't that be a nice "problem" to have?). The important action is going to be sitting down and getting a handle on these items. You want to really understand how your money is working for you, where it is going, and to ensure you are not overspending. In essence, you want to ensure you are not spending tomorrow's money today, as that's no different than spending on a credit card, and it's a mess you will find very difficult to get out of if it gets too bad.

It really isn't my place to tell you how to build your company, I am simply trying to help you with your credit, so I do advocate getting your finances right—all of your finances, and that includes your own company. This will include taking the time to really understand how your cash flows work in your business along with your personal finances. There are all kinds of resources that can assist you in this, including your bookkeeper and your accounting software. The best place to start is by making sure you aren't spending money you don't have, even if it's in your bank account, and the only way you can truly understand this is to get a handle on your cash flow statement—what is coming in, what is going out, and how you are truly defining income in your business. Getting a handle on these items are the only way to start in getting a handle on your business. It's all about understanding your cash flows.

# 36

# Build Equity

One of the last items I want to touch on briefly is about building equity in your company. All too often, smaller entrepreneurs and newer companies have a tendency to distribute all the profits of the business to the owners. *I want to encourage you not to do this*. You need to leave something in your business, even after taxes are paid. This starts to build savings and equity in your company. It puts a tangible net worth into your company. Why should you do this? Well, if you don't put money into your business, or in essence "lend" yourself this money, why should any banker, investor, or anyone else? Furthermore, if you are not building the net worth of the company than you aren't building any long-term value in your company. This doesn't have to sit as cash in your bank or as straight-up investments; it could be infrastructure, buildings, and so on—anything that ends up bringing value to your company. The idea here is that you are not pulling everything out of the business, even if you could. Instead, you are leaving profit in the business. Realistically, unless you need every dollar out of the business, the taxation level for your company is better than you taking it out personally anyway.

So, who can help you with this? Remember that bookkeeper? Well, you may need someone with upgraded skills for this, such as an accountant or an accounting firm that can help you, and you will likely have to pay good money for the advice you get, but it should be worth it in the longer term. The best person is going to be someone who doesn't work in your firm, so they will be a bit more objective than anyone on your staff can be.

This leads me to the last item for your business I wanted to mention in the next and final chapter of this book.

# 37

# Other Resources

Resources. Some of the best resources you need to have are good accounting resources. Yes, you will need to have a software program, and maybe a bookkeeper, but eventually a good full-blown accountant is going to be of great help to you— someone who can help you make some of these decisions and plans I have covered. I'd encourage you to keep them honest by checking what they are charging you every so often. You can do this by having an open tender with a few other firms every few years, say every five or ten years, just to keep them honest and ensure you aren't being overcharged. Like my earlier story , sometimes you can be forced into the situation, but it's better to just go ahead and check things out every once in a while.

The other resources out there are books, such as *Profit First* by Mike Michalowicz, but there are so many other books you can read to help you on your journey. I'd be arrogant to think this is the only book you need to get yourself sorted out for the future. Books like *The Wealthy Barber*,[8] *The Wealthy Barber Returns*,[9] *The Money Code*,[10] and many others have been written to help you fix up your finances. Every one of these books are

---

[8]  https://www.amazon.com/Wealthy-Barber-Updated-3rd-Commonsense/dp/0761513116

[9]  http://www.wealthybarber.com

[10]  https://greenleafbookgroup.com/titles/the-money-code

there to help YOU turn things around, so read them and pick out the items that work for you and run with them. Not every situation is going to be valid for you, so treat it like a grocery store.

# 38

# In Conclusion

This book has been a labor of love. I wrote it because I saw so many people across so many countries hurting from a lack of credit, no savings, a negative credit report, and ultimately a lack of hope. This is my way of trying to change that. I have personally used the tactics in this book, which is why I wrote it. They are just as valid now as when I used them twenty years ago.

Temptation abounds to put you under by giving you access to too much credit too easily and in the wrong forms. It's my hope that the strategies in this book will help you take a chunk out of your mountain of debt and to lessen some of the stress you may be under.

In full disclosure, my business is a money lending business, and we try to do this as ethically as possible for entrepreneurs like yourself, balancing the need for credit with your ability to repay. We never try to offer more than you can corporately afford to pay back as it's not in our best interest to do that. Every product we have released has always been for the purpose of helping you to do better, whether it's leasing, loans, car lending, or charge cards. Yes, my company actually offers a charge card product like the one I described earlier, and no it's not the one I used so many years ago, but when we embarked on this book project, the charge card was one of the main drivers for releasing it. Our goal is to change the lives of 1,000,000 entrepreneurs. We want to help you succeed in growing your business so you can help other people, your staff, your family, and your vendors succeed. We believe that together we all achieve more and we all succeed if we help each other succeed. A rising tide lifts all boats!

There was no book out there like this when I needed it so many years ago, and I truly hope it has been helpful to you. I also hope my personal story has helped you see the changes you need to make, and I invite you to contact us at www. scorebydnd.com or via email at info@scorebydnd.com. We are at your disposal in any way we can be helpful.

Just remember the plan will work if you work the plan, and that for you the best is yet to come!

## CALL TO ACTION

DND Finance has numerous credit products available that are geared for small and medium businesses, including leases, loans, car loans, truck financing, and the charge cards described in this book for both personal and corporate use. Feel free to contact us at our corporate site, www.dndf.business, to learn more, or visit the site for this book at www.scorebydnd.com/debttowealth.

www.ingramcontent.com/pod-product-compliance
Lightning Source LLC
Chambersburg PA
CBHW071701210326
41597CB00017B/2281